Echoes From a Cc

© David

Foreword

This book is a continuation of my previous book 'What Has He Done Now? It has stories from the early sixties right up to the present day. It isn't a biography as such, but more a collection of random thoughts and feelings about life in and around the area of my birth. It is a catalogue of sentiments, both sad and funny. The fact that I was born and raised in Leigh, Lancashire is incidental. My childhood was like millions of other children's lives in Britain. Some of the words we used may differ, but the story of the streets remains the same.

It was about making do with what we had. I have tried not to eulogise about life back then. Very often the good old days weren't particularly good at all! The book is not in praise of days gone by, but neither is it in condemnation of it. I have tried to make it an honest reflection of how things were - for me anyway. The book contains several reflections from my childhood, but thoughts from the present day. As the title suggests, all these tales are echoes from a cobbled street; for it was on such a street I was born.

Shove Up a Bit

A couch, a settee, a sofa - call it what you will. We all had one.
Posh folks with bigger houses had a few. We just had the one,
together with a matching armchair. We had a tiled fireplace with a
blazing coal fire burning in the grate. One of the few luxuries as
Dad worked for the coal board, so we got concessionary coal (which
was kept below the stairs and was accessed through the kitchen).
It was a good old, North West, two up, two down with an outside
lavatory and no bathroom. I digress. Back to the couch.

The couch was designed to accommodate three people, but I have
seen it hold up to seven kids. The seat cushions were removable,
and lots of stuff found its way down the back of the cushions.
Whenever one turned up on a bonfire in November, we would go
'couch diving'. Rummaging inside the sofa lining and down the
back, to find long-lost bits of loose change. I remember the cry
going up from one of the lads 'I've found threppy' meaning
threepence. Quite a sum of money back then for a kid.

For some odd reason, Mam kept old newspapers underneath the
cushions. She wasn't one of these weird hoarders that you see on
telly. They were used to light the fire. In pre toilet roll days
they also found their way into the outside 'petty' where they were
cut into squares and hung upon a nail on the door. Mam also
wrapped potato peelings with it. 'It stops them smelling' she used
to say. It didn't work. Everyone's bin stank on warm days.

The couch was also a makeshift bed when I was ill. Being ill was
almost a treat. Being tucked up on the couch while wearing my jim-
jams, eating boiled eggs and toast soldiers, or better still,
drinking Lucozade, of which the bottle came wrapped in yellow
coloured, cellophane wrapping. It crackled as you unwrapped it
like a big yellow sweet. There was also the telly in the same
room. Everyone else would moan and carp on because they had to sit
on the floor, but Mam would say 'It's only what I would do for you
if you were ill'. The couch was the focal point of family
entertainment. It's where we watched our luxurious 14" black and
white television with just two channels. BBC and ITV. We had to
rent a new one when BBC2 came along, because ours only had 405
lines, and you had to have 625 lines and a new style aerial to
watch BBC2. This turned out to be utter crap, but it was an excuse
to rent a new, bigger telly. We hired ours from Red Arrow. They
gave you a little rubber doll of an Indian (or Native Americans as
we should now call them). It had holes to insert five little
rubber feathers. You earned these by introducing friends and
family. Each one that signed up, you earned a feather. Fill all
five, and they gave you £5. A brilliant piece of marketing. We
filled up two dolls.

The couch came into its own on Christmas morning. It's where
everyone sat to open their presents, which were then played with
on the rug, in front of the fire. It would be festooned with

pieces of torn wrapping paper, which would also find their way beneath the cushions. The fire would be lit with it on Boxing Day morning.

The couch would also be the seat of honour for any visiting guests. 'Come on David, get up and let Mr and Mrs Roberts sit down'. The couch also doubled up as the dock. Any miscreants (usually me) were sat down on the couch and questioned about who they had been with, what they had done, and was it true what she had heard. I always owned up to it because, 1) I usually had committed the misdemeanour, and 2) I got treated more leniently if I owned up to it and threw myself upon their mercy. If I saw Dad trying to stifle back a laugh, I knew I was home and dry. If I heard the words 'You little bugger' Mam would usually send me to bed. The worst was when Dad would say 'I'm very disappointed in you'. Dad was my hero. I always wanted to live up to my hero. This rejection was usually punishment enough and would reduce me to tears.

The sofa also became a psychiatrists couch, where counselling sessions were held. One of Mam's friends would be sniffling into a hankie, with Mam offering advice, such as 'All men are swines. You have to teach them that no means no'. It's only years later the meaning of those words came back to me. I suddenly spat out my tea and burst out laughing. Everyone thought I had lost the plot, but when the penny drops, you react.

The couch was also packed on Friday nights when the neighbours came round, and Dad played the piano. All three seats and both arms had bottoms on them. Renditions of all the old favourites, like Begin the Beguine', 'Roll Out The Barrel', and 'The Whiffenpoof Song', but the one that always got the old ladies crying into their stout was 'Nobody's Child'. When Dad was out, and Mam was in the kitchen, occasionally the couch was moved back to make room for my two sisters to 'bop' to their records. Bopping is that dance where the girl twirls underneath the boy's arm, like those old black and white films of American soldiers at a dance. They even taught me how to do it, but I was just too short. On infrequent occasions, Dad would come home from the pub and see the girls bopping. He would smile, change the record and have a little dance with Mam, and tell us 'This is proper dancing. You get to hold your little sweetie-pie'. Everyone would groan and say 'Oh, Dad!!!!'.

I always feel that when you move into a house, it doesn't become a home until you carry in the couch and set up the telly. Only then does it become liveable. The sofa is the most British of institutions and the glue that holds a family together. They can be used to hide behind when the Daleks came on Dr Who; they can be used to be kissed, cuddled and made love on, they can hold a rackload of kids to watch Blue Peter, they can be used for a lovely afternoon siesta, a whole plethora of things. The couch is the place of tears and laughter, fear and love. It is comfort and refuge. It is the epicentre of that which we call home. The couch is the real British hero - as Tiny Tim might have said '...and God bless them, every one'.

A Lancashire Weaver

This place might be haunted
the ghost hunter said.
'Midst the dust and the grime
walk the feet of the dead.
The machines now stand idle.
Looms clatter no more.
There's a stack of old bobbins
piled up by the door.
I remember my Mam
she worked here, so she said
A Lancashire weaver
but now she is dead.
Along with this mill
and along with the dreams
of working mill lasses
and their jobs, so it seems.
We once wove the best
cotton cloth in the world.
But now that's all gone;
on the scrap heap been hurled.
The clatter of clogs
on the old cobbled street.
The humdrum staccato
from thousands of feet.
Tough work and much hardship
and many a care.
Folks they got by
for brass, it was rare.
But still, we had pride,
By Christ, did we ever!
Will it ever come back?
The answer is NEVER!
This place might be haunted
the ghost hunter said.
'Midst the dust and the grime
walk the feet of the dead.
I'm glad that my Mam
never saw it this way.
Out in all weathers,
came here every day.
When this closed down
she had already died.
Perhaps just as well.
She'd have bloody well cried.

Fashion - 1965

I had an auntie who was addicted to knitting. I'm sure that she
could still knit while she was asleep. People would donate wool to
her out of kindness, as she always had that haunted, hungry look
in her eyes when she was coming down off the wool. She would buy
old hand-knitted jumpers at jumble sales just to pull them apart
and knit them back into a jumper, but one that was far, far worse.

Practice never seemed to bring the much-promised perfection. She
wasn't good at 'V' necks, or any necks come to that matter. She
never used any patterns, and everything was in plain stitch. She
would have been much in demand by the film industry for making
primitive, authentic-looking, period knitwear, that period being
somewhere when people didn't give a sod what they looked like. Mam
once told her (a stupid thing to do) that she was off to the shops
to buy me a school jumper. Auntie said 'I'll make him one too'.
The look of alarm upon my face couldn't have been plainer. 'Awwww,
Mam. Don't let her', I said, which resulted in a slap round the
back of my head. Mother quickly explained that I meant that I
didn't want her going to all that trouble. I got as far as saying
'No, Mam it will....' before earning another crack round the back
of the head and being whisked off to the shops. Once outside, Mam
said 'You don't half show me up at times'. I answered her by
saying 'You don't have to go outside wearing it'. I could see the
sadness and the sympathy in her eyes.

Auntie didn't let me down. Mam brought it home. Auntie had lived
up to every last dropped stitch of her reputation. Dad put down
his newspaper and said 'That bag looks heavy. Let's have a look at
it'. Mam dragged half a stone of knitted wool from out of her bag.
The arms seemed to go on forever, but that was nothing when
compared to her failed attempt at a 'V' neck. I saw Dad's lips
move. He didn't speak the words, but he clearly said the 'F' word.
He walked around it a couple of times like it was an exhibition at
Tate Modern, before saying, 'When did he become a hunchback?' Mam
thought this irreverent and an act of ungratefulness, but I saw
her titter. 'What do you think, Seth?' she asked. Dad answered
with 'It looks like someone knitted a jumper and it had a stroke'.
I chipped in with 'Don't make me wear it, Mam', almost tearfully.
'Don't worry son, I have to own you. You don't have to wear it'
Dad replied, much to my relief. Dad then winked at Mam and said
'Mind you, it would save us a few bob, and you will probably grow
into it. Let's see what it looks like on'. The only way I would
have grown into it would be to become an orangutan. I put up the
expected resistance, but finally, put it on.

The 'V' neck was magnificent. It was of different lengths on each
side and finished somewhere around three inches from my navel. The
hem touched my knees and the sleeves, well, the sleeves had a life
of their own. The right arm was around ten inches too long and the
left arm only around six. Dad collapsed into his chair and laughed
so loud that he broke wind, which set him off again. After he had

composed himself and wiped the tears from his eyes, he perpetrated the ultimate betrayal in my eyes. 'Send him round wearing it, to thank her', he said. Then both he and Mam burst out laughing. Mam could see the look of sheer panic on my face and said 'Don't worry love. He's joking'.

Dad said 'Take it off and let me try it on'. This had now turned into party mode. It was a little snug around the midriff, but the length looked about right. 'This is grand, it will keep my backside warm too' he said. Then pulled it down over his buttocks. Dad saw the expression on Mam's face change. He turned around to see auntie looking in through the kitchen window. She entered the kitchen, and said 'Now Seth, I knitted that for our David, but you look GORGEOUS in it'. Mam stood beside her in complete agreement, and said 'That's what I thought, and our David has a school jumper'. Then Mam stitched Dad up like an absolute kipper. She said 'He says he's going out tonight and taking your Percy for a pint and seeing as he likes it so much, he is wearing it'. Then added 'Isn't that right, Seth?' Dad nodded like the condemned man that he was.

After Auntie had left, Dad said 'I'd forgotten what a malicious sod you can be at times' then kissed her cheek. I believe the last time it ever saw the light of day again was when knitted dresses were in fashion, and my sister put a belt around her waist and wore it as such. Even then, Mam said she looked ridiculous and made her take it off.

1962 - Carol Singing.

'Shall we allow girls with us then?' Graham asked. No one seemed keen. 'Why do you want....girls' Michael answered. The pause was because he could hardly utter the words without gagging! 'Because girls sing nice, so we might get more money' he answered.

Carol singing was taken seriously in our little gang, and although the angelic sound of seven-year-old children's voices may be appealing - it is appealing only if they are all in the same key! Reluctantly, we all agreed. Finding girls as a sixteen-year-old was terrible enough. It was no different as a seven-year-old. Graham, being our elected spokesman was delegated to approach any wild and roaming packs of females that we encountered upon the frozen plains of Lancashire.

'There's a pair o'er yonder' Brian said. Indeed there were. They were called Kim and Anne. 'Do you two want for't come carol singin' with us lot?' He asked. Quick as a flash, Kim answered with 'Well I don't know. Let's hear yer sing first'. We launched into 'Once in Royal David's City'. Unfortunately, I started it off in too high a key. Once we got to the line 'Mary was that mother mild. Jesus Christ, her little child' we were straining and red-faced. The notes were so high only dogs could hear us. The two girls dissolved into laughter. They weren't just laughing, they were on the point of quite literally wetting themselves.

We didn't wait around for the inevitable answer and shuffled off. Everyone was blaming me for picking the key. The next thing, Kim and Anne caught up with us. 'Sorry for laughing, but it was funny' Anne said. Soon we were all laughing. They agreed to come along with us, and we all shared a copy of something called 'The Little Book of Christmas Songs' that had the words in it. Even then, I had ideas above my station. I didn't understand harmonies in the least, but I had an idea. We boys would start the carol and sing the first verse. Then we would unleash our secret weapon. The girls would join us on the second verse - kapow! The impact would be spectacular. Inside our minds, we were already spending the riches.

We all met on the street corner later that evening. Darkness had fallen. On all those Christmas cards with carol singers on them, they had a picture of the choir. One of them would be holding a beautiful, Victorian lantern with a candle in it. I brought along an old paraffin storm lamp that we kept lit in the outside toilet to stop it freezing in winter. We all agreed it looked 'proper nice'. We turned up at the first front door. I launched into Silent Night, and for once, we were all roughly in the same key. I glowed with pride. Then it came time for the showstopper. It was time for the girls to join in. What happened next I will never forget as long as my memory persists. The noises that issued forth I have only heard replicated coming from a pork abattoir. It wasn't even in any discernible key. It was somewhere in the cracks

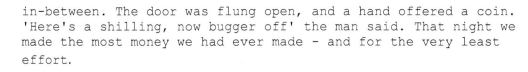

in-between. The door was flung open, and a hand offered a coin. 'Here's a shilling, now bugger off' the man said. That night we made the most money we had ever made - and for the very least effort.

King Coal - 1960's

Coming from the North West, there were many colliery spoil heaps.
We knew them as rucks. Huge, austere, imposing piles that
dominated the skyline and glowered down upon the streets and
houses below. Some caught fire due to spontaneous ignition. They
smouldered deep inside, occasionally erupting in plumes of smoke
from the surface. These unlikely places were our adventure
playgrounds. These were our hills and our mountains. Their lofty
heights afforded us some spectacular views of our little towns and
villages. Amongst all the waste and spoil could be seen the small,
glistening black diamonds of coal. In harder times some would pick
through the spoil heaps for these little pieces of coal to heat
their homes. It was called 'Coal Picking' (for quite obvious
reasons). Often these sacks of coal were carted home across the
crossbar of a bicycle, like panniers on a pack mule, or an old
pram would be used. The spoil heaps being the property of the
mining company, this was somewhat illegal.

To us, these rucks were just our playground. The sides of the
rucks sloped off at anything from around forty-five degrees or
steeper. These were our all-year-round toboggan slopes. We would
use bits of old corrugated tin turned up at the front, or better
still, a short length of colliery conveyor belting. The more
adventurous crouched down on their haunches with one foot in front
of the other and went down that way. Eventually, everyone came a
cropper and went sliding down on their backsides, tearing holes in
the seat of their trousers, and putting gravel rash down their
legs.

We once found an old, cast iron, enamelled bath. We smashed the
decorative claw feet off it to eliminate any drag on the surface
of the rucks and used that as our vehicle. It could fit three kids
in it comfortably. Four at a very tight squeeze. The journey down
was fast, exhilarating, often very bumpy and with no guarantee of
a safe arrival at the bottom. We once spotted a gully in the rucks
due to rain erosion. It went down straight for a while and then
curved off near the bottom. Just beyond this was a brook around
ten feet wide. It seemed that the gully would carry us off at the
bottom, thus avoiding the brook. Unfortunately for us, it did no
such thing. We hit the curve at the bottom at some speed and were
immediately launched into the air, landing with an enormous
splash, right into the orange, iron oxide water. We all emerged
looking like we had had a spray tan without removing our clothes
first. Mam was NOT happy!

At the bottom of most rucks were smaller, shallower hills. These
were fabulous for riding our bikes around. We planned little race
tracks around them. I suppose we were the forerunners of the BMX
and mountain bike brigade. Some were perfect for getting both
wheels off the ground. I remember launching off one of these jumps
and hanging in the air for an extraordinary amount of time (or so
it felt). I let with a thud several feet further on. The impact

knocked me forward and onto the crossbar. I bobbled along with my testicles jarring on the crossbar for several yards, before falling sideways and rolling around on the ground clutching my groin and doing what can only be described as 'silent screaming'. That is when you hit that point where the pain is just too much to bear, and you do an impression of 'The Scream' by Edvard Munch. Mouth wide open but no sound coming out. My friends were also rolling around on the ground - but through tears of laughter. They then started offering me 'helpful' advice, such as 'Hey, Hayzee. Don't rub 'em, count 'em'. Oddly enough I failed to see the humour in the situation. I did answer them with a stream of very colourful language and brought each one of their parent's marital situations into doubt at the time of their birth.

After a while, they helped me up and did sympathise a little. 'What did it feel like?' one of them asked. 'Oh brilliant. I'm just popping back up the slope to try it again' I sarcastically replied. Before adding 'What do you bloody THINK it felt like?' but to no reply. That part of our little circuit was christened 'Hayzee's Leap' after that.

Amongst those smaller hills, we dug little craters further down into existing depressions and put discarded bits of wood and old tin sheets over the top of them. These became our dens. I remember one luxury model that we had. It contained a length of old drain pipe sitting above a box of bricks and resting on a piece of mesh. This made our chimney. Around the sides and on top of the mesh we placed sods of grass. The chimney worked a treat A good up-draught. These were our illicit smoking dens. (Yes, even as kids we tried such things). Mostly though, we just sat inside them and had a giggle. There's something about fire and little boys. It attracts us in a similar manner as a moth to a candle flame. Even today, I can happily sit around a garden fire.

This may sound in some way grim and from the pages of some Orwellian industrial nightmare scenario. It was far from it. These spoil heaps were surrounded by some lovely bits of countryside. We had a few areas of mixed woodland where trees had reclaimed industrial land that had once been theirs. There were ponds and pit lodges that were filled with a healthy population of wildfowl and hungry perch that were only too willing to accept our bait. Be it a maggot or a juicy earthworm. This was our little paradise, complete with our man-made mountains. It was home to us, and we were borne of this landscape. Sons of pit-men and mill lasses. Absolutely nothing career-wise was expected of us. This made many of us try all the harder if only to say 'Sod you, posh folks. Here comes some Northern grit'.

Coal Face Warriors

Where are you now, you collier lads.
You men who dug and won the coal.
Aye, WON! - it didn't dig itself.
They had to go down that dark hole.

Some days they went down in the dark
and in the dark came up again.
Down to the pit no matter what.
In any weather snow or rain.

So many men, they met their fate
deep down in that dark, dismal place.
So many died, brave collier lads
when hewing coal from off the face.

They dug like rats to win those gems
and then a pit prop it would crack.
The last sound that they ever heard
A mother's son not coming back.

By the thousands they went down
and by the hundreds, sadly died.
So many children went without
the bitter tears their widows cried.

It is now but a memory.
The pit head wheels no longer turn.
From Germany our coal now comes.
It's foreign coal that we now burn.

Where are their monuments, these men
these warriors who hewed our coal.
Behind their banners they did march
into the past, and to the dole.

Remember them, these warriors
who dug for coal with pick and spade.
Our wealth upon their shoulders borne
by the sacrifices that they made.

When I Was Six

It was the wedding of one of my cousins. They dolled me up in a little suit and a dickie-bow (I jest you not....and no, I don't have any pictures). It was a rather posh affair. Three bridesmaids, and me carrying a cushion with two rings on it. I didn't trust them perched on top of the cushion, so instead of carrying it like a tray as intended, I stuck one hand underneath and one hand on top. It looked like I was about to drop-kick it like a rugby ball.

It came to my part in the proceedings, but I was staring in mesmerised fashion at this rather gruesome picture of some beardy bloke nailed to some wood. I was pushed forward by one of the bridesmaids. I said 'Oh aye, sorry, 'ere they are'. Mam didn't look the best part pleased, but everyone else was cooing and saying 'Awwww bless him'. I suppose I was there for the cute factor.

After all the palaver was over and they had been covered in big handfuls of coloured paper shaped like horseshoes and hearts, we headed off to the reception. On the way there in the taxi I said 'Mam, Mam, Mam....will there be sausage rolls and then jelly for afters?' She said 'I wouldn't imagine so'. The day just seemed to be getting worse, and my dickie-bow was being pushed upwards by my starched shirt. At times it looked like I had a purple, comedy moustache.

We arrived at the venue, and it looked really posh. There were all these miserable looking blokes walking around with drinks on trays. They were calling everyone Sir or Madam. I never got offered one though. A while later a waitress brought me a glass of orange juice. One of the blokes then started hitting something that looked like a brass dustbin lid, then it was time to sit down.

We all found our tables. We had our names written on little cards. Mine said 'Master David Hayes'. I said 'Whoa look, Mam, look, look. MASTER David Hayes' she smiled. 'Can I keep it Mam?' I asked her. She told me that she would put it in her handbag. In front of me was this white cloth inside a little ring thing. Mam told me that this was a napkin. 'What's it for Mam?' I asked her. She told me I had to drape it over my knees. The napkin was so big that to a casual observer it looked like I was wearing a white cotton dress. 'Now what Mam?' I asked her. 'Just leave it there while you eat' she replied.

They then brought us these shrimps in some pink gunk, and in a glass. They had also shoved some bits of lettuce in there. 'Can you eat that Mam?' I asked her. She told me that I could and that it was called a prawn cocktail. I picked up a spoon from the table and dug in. Just then I noticed that everyone else was using a little fork. 'Oh well,' I thought to myself and soldiered on. Mam

quickly took the napkin off my knee and pushed it down the front
of my waistcoat. Just in time to stop big, pink blobs from
covering the front of me. After that, we had roast chicken with
posh looking potatoes, carrots and some long, green, pointy
things. 'What are them things Mam?' I asked her. She said they
were called something like 'A Sparrows Grass'. They tasted
horrible, so I left them. Everyone else was cooing over them.
Weird!!!

Then my cousin and her bloke cut into this massive white cake with
something that looked like a sword and everyone started taking
photographs. I had no idea why. I have seen Mam cutting cake loads
of times. Then everyone clapped. It was a total puzzlement to me.
It looked easy enough, and two of them were holding the sword..ah
well!!

Then it was time for pudding. 'Trifle yayyyy' I said as they
placed the bowl in front of me. I licked clean the spoon I had
eaten the prawns with and got stuck in. God, it was gorgeous.
After that, it all got a bit silly. My cousin and her bloke danced
in the middle of the dance floor like they had both had a stroke
and were supporting each other, while all the ladies started
crying and saying things like 'Ee bless them. Don't they look
happy together'?

Wedding of the Month

Church pews they begin to fill.
Dad still blanching at the bill.
The Groom he will soon take a Wife.
You can cut the tension with a knife.
Platitudes and gratitude.
Relatives with attitude.
A dress of white? - was that wise?
Her belly it is such a size!
Wedding march, the bride in view.
Very soon both say "I DO"
Children fidget, mothers chide.
'Sir, you may now kiss the bride'.
Off they go to the Parish Hall.
Music, dancing, have a ball!
The tables groan with food galore.
Children sliding on the floor.
Mothers glare a withering frown.
Pick up their kids and dust them down.
The band strikes up, a tenor croons.
Uncle, PLEASE don't play the spoons!
The bride and groom for photos, kissing.
The Best man and the bridesmaid missing?
Time to cut the wedding cake,
though the silver handled knife's a fake!
Then the last waltz starts to play
and very soon they're on their way.
Old folks talk of weddings past.
The sceptics wonder will it last?
Then off they go, this man and wife
to parenthood, and their new life.

Bath Night and Grooming Techniques - 1960s

Dad was lucky in some ways. He had the 'luxury' of the pit-head
baths. He could take a hot shower at the end of each and every
working day. We had to resort to the tin bath. This was stored in
the toilet at the bottom of the yard. When needed, it was carried
into the house and placed in front of the kitchen fire. It was
then filled, by way of a galvanised bucket, with lashings of hot
water. The back door was the old-fashioned door-latch kind. The
only time this was ever locked (by way of two heavy door bolts),
was during bath night. The neighbours had the 'knock and enter'
mentality. They would knock, and then shout round the door 'It's
only me', before walking in. I think it was mother who first
learned this lesson - the hard way!

Bath nights were usually on a Sunday. Yes, we only had a bath once
a week. The time and expense of heating up the water and the sheer
slog of filling and then emptying the tub made it the logical
outcome. So, you would probably think that each of us would take a
bath in clean water. You would be wrong. All four of us (my
Mother, my two sisters and myself) would take a bath in the same
water. It was a hierarchy system of eldest first. In went Mam for
a good soak, followed then in turn by my two sisters. By the time
it was my turn the water was virtually cold, scummy and most
uninviting.

My younger sister once waited until she could hear me splashing
around in the bath before she shouted through the door 'I had a
wee in that'. She then ran away chuckling. I told my mother about
this afterwards. Her reaction was precious. She said to me 'Ah
well, think yourself lucky. It would have warmed the water up a
bit'.

Once this ritual was over, the bath was emptied with the same tin
bucket until there was only a couple of inches left in it. The tub
was then dragged outside and emptied down the grid. It wasn't
completely devoid of any comfort or luxury. Anyone who hasn't
dried themselves while standing on a peg rug, in front of a
roaring coal fire, is missing something sumptuous.

After my bath, I would put on my pyjamas, and dressing gown and
Mam would make the bath-night treat. A mug of cocoa each. I was
then allowed a little television before being sent upstairs to
bed. During the six 'non-bath' days, we had what was known as a
flannel wash. This was precisely what it sounds like. The Belfast
sink in the kitchen was partially filled with hot water and using
a bar of Fairy soap and flannel, you gave yourself a good body
wash. At least with the flannel wash, we had the luxury of clean
water each time. For some reason, particular attention was always
paid to my neck. Mam would say 'Have you washed your neck
properly? Let me have a look'. No matter how well I washed it, she
would always take a look and then say 'Hmmm, it will do I
suppose'. Surgeons scrubbed their hands with less enthusiasm than

I washed my neck. It's one of the small hang-ups that I still have. If I were knocked down by a bus, I would imagine my mother looking down from above and saying 'Well thank god he has clean underwear and he's washed his neck'.

Two or three times a week mother would also sit me down on a kitchen chair and start looking through my hair as if we were chimpanzees, and she was grooming me. She would also drag the nit comb through my hair a few times to check for nit eggs. Fortunately, I only ever caught them once, and that was through playing rugby league at school. I was in the front row in the scrum, and our heads would often rub together. The look of abject horror on my mother's face was a picture. You would think I had come home with rabies! There then followed a prolonged session of washing my head in some special shampoo and an intensive going-over with the nit comb. My head was stinging by the time she had done.

We were all the same in our street. No one had much of anything. No one worried too much if jumpers had leather patches sewn onto the elbows, or even darned with different coloured wool. Our clothes may have been old, but both the clothes and our little bodies were clean. The sheets on the washing line were as white as driven snow. My mother used to say 'You can tell a lot about a woman by looking on her clothesline'.

I suppose what I am trying to say is, that we had pride. As neighbours, we also helped each other out. This was brought home to me when Dad had a stroke. Every one of the neighbours knocked on our door to ask if they could help and if we needed anything. I make it sound whimsical and romantic. It was far from it. It was gritty, tough and very real. We may have been poor in money, but we were rich in love. Our parents gave us two things. Love and freedom. We didn't want to be inside the house, and they didn't want us there. 'Go out and play' was a phrase that I heard every day. I don't miss the deprivation and the surrounding squalor of the neighbourhood. I don't miss the lack of any form of modern digital entertainment, but I do miss the contentment.

There was a sense of knowing what was affordable and what wasn't. The 'never never' was for bigger things like the cooker or the washing machine. There was a 'Clubman' who sold goods such as shoes and clothes and you paid so much a week until they were paid off. It was all recorded in his ledger that he carried around with him on his rounds. The fear of the bailiff and the lack of money stopped any of us getting into debt. There was no easy credit and plastic back then. I don't even remember my Mam and Dad having a cheque book. I wouldn't swap my past. Not for a king's ransom.

A Mother's Advice

I no longer have the will
To tell you how I feel.
Seems I just can't find the strength
to let my heart reveal,
the way I'm feeling when I see
the way you lead your life.
The way that all material things
seem to cause you strife.

You say your phone it is too old.
You say your car is too.
You say that being ordinary
makes you feel so blue.
I wish that I could lead you back
to when you were a child.
When adventure meant the park.
When life was far more mild.

When monsters lived beneath your bed
I made them go away.
When kisses made things better
with many hugs each day.
Did I teach you nothing?
Where did I go so wrong?
Cast your mind back to the time
when life was like a song.

The things that matter you can't buy.
You learn these things with age.
Life gives you reminders
as you turn each page.
Count your blessings one by one
as each one does arrive.
Celebrate the gifts you have
Remember, YOU'RE ALIVE

Sweet Sunday.

Delicate tendrils of aroma from a roasting joint, slowly cooking in the oven, drifted out of the kitchen window and drew us back to the blessed warmth of the kitchen. This was all part of the carnival atmosphere and the precursor to the main meal of the week, Sunday dinner. We didn't need calling to the table twice.

Mam would take the joint from the oven and lift it out of the roasting tin, then put it onto a willow pattern meat charger. She then poured the juices from the roast into a jug and made the gravy with it. That gravy was a real work of art. A perfect accompaniment to her Yorkshire Puddings. Small individual ones made with one of those tin cupcake trays. She would buy goose fat from the butchers, especially for the purpose. They were as light as promises and crisp to the bite - but like promises, they were also easily broken. Crisp on the outside, but soft as angel feathers inside. The gravy would be liberally splashed over the meat, boiled potatoes and carrots, and would sit in little pools inside the Yorkshire Puddings.

A large, dark brown teapot sat in the centre of the table alongside all the condiments. On Sunday, we would be a little posh and drink from bone china cups and saucers. There was a plate with buttered slices of bread. For some reason back then, every meal had to have bread. This was indeed the one, big family meal. It was the unwritten rule, 'Thou shalt attend'.

If the money would stretch to it, Mam preferred to buy a nice joint of beef. I suppose with it being more expensive than pork, we felt like we were a little bit posher. That said, I preferred the pork. You got more of it for the money, and the crackling - oh my!! If heaven had a flavour, it would be pork crackling.

After the meal, we would sit in a state of stupor, like over-stuffed soft toys at the table. The occasional appreciative belch, and the admonishing words of mother saying 'Say I beg your pardon after you burp. You weren't dragged up'. Even though we were quite replete, there always came exactly the same question 'What for pudding, Mam?'

I always hoped she would say 'It's your favourite. Heinz sponge pudding and custard'. These puddings were cooked in the tin in a pan of boiling water. The tin would do a little tap dance as it rattled around in the big, aluminium pan. Being honest, I didn't mind what she said. There was always a pudding of some sort. Her rice puddings were a delight. We would fight for who got the skin from the top of it.

When I think of Sundays, I always think of good food, sunshine, and the love that was there in abundance around the kitchen table. I know it can't have always been sunny, but in my mind, it was. Sunday indeed was a day of rest. I remember us all listening to

Sing Something Simple on the Light Programme on the radio. This later became Radio 2. I pretended to hate all the songs and moaned about how old-fashioned they were. Secretly, I quite enjoyed them, but I had to keep my 'street cred' intact!

I was then packed off to go and play outside. This wasn't in any way a punishment. We loved the rough and tumble of the street games. Later on, there was the old haunted goldfish bowl in the corner of the room - our telly. It would be in the mid-sixties when Batman came to UK television. We even started sentences with the word 'Holy' like Robin did to Batman. He would say things like 'Holy bat-catastrophe Batman'. It impressed us no end, as did the cartoon captions in the fight scenes, saying things like 'KAPOW' and 'THWACK'. We honestly did catch Batmania.

The only programme to surpass this was Dr Who. When I watch those old episodes today, I chuckle to myself. Back then though, they were genuinely terrifying. Especially when those metallic voiced marauders appeared upon the scene. The legendary Daleks. We would all wander around saying 'I am a Dalek. I am a Dalek'. The irony is that I don't believe those words were ever spoken by them. The other word we said was though. That being 'EXTERMINATE'. As kids, I think we all hid behind the sofa when the Daleks showed up. I think the first time they were seen was during the tenure of the first doctor, William Hartnell.

Sunday to us wasn't about church. I suppose we were a little bit heathen. I think I did go to Sunday School for a short while, but only to get me from under mother's feet. It thankfully didn't last long. The only times we went to church were for weddings, christenings and funerals. Or 'Hatch, match and dispatch' as Dad always called these events.

Sunday was like the treat at the end of the week. It was when the ice cream man toured our street. Sunday was like the welcoming kiss after a long week of hard work. It was also bath night. I have memories of sitting in front of the fire in my dressing gown and pyjamas with wet hair. We were allowed to stay up to watch some telly, then packed off to bed, as it was school the next day. Sundays were days of laughter, love and full bellies.

Many of my childhood memories are rooted in the fertile soil of such days. We couldn't always afford the latest toys. Money was very much at a premium, but we were loved. Not the mushy love, where people fire off the 'three little words' at random at the drop of a hat. I can't ever remember telling Mam and Dad that I loved them. It was just taken as read. We had the practical love. We were fed, watered, clothed and given the occasional cuddle, but on occasion, a hand across our backside when it was merited. In short, we felt secure. This is a commodity that seems to be sadly lacking today.

No dark clouds dare pass across those horizons. Those golden meadows of my childhood dreams. Love was not a word often used. It was like oxygen. We just absorbed it and breathed it in without even realising. It was just there. Common, plentiful and freely given. In fact, there was always some to spare for others. It is the ones who have the least that more commonly give the most.

Outgrown clothing was handed on to other neighbours. Perfectly pressed and laundered, but given with such dismissive words as 'It'll do for your Peter to play out in'. It was almost like a game. The answer would arrive along the lines of 'Don't be daft. I'll put this away for Sunday best'. Two words that fit together like strawberries and cream, or apple pie and custard. The words 'Sunday' and 'Best. Because Sundays were the best. The very best of all.

The Blank Page

Look into those children's eyes
and see the trust and love inside.
All that hope and shining dreams
inside their little souls abide.
When they ask you 'What is love?'
Don't show them films from Hollywood.
Tell them about sacrifice.
Give examples of both right and good.
Tell them love it does forgive.
Tell them love's an open door.
Tell them patient smiles are love.
Forgive them as you did before.
Feed their minds with happiness.
Slow to chide and quick to bless.
Love it is the only choice.
Love will always bring success.

Free Gift Inside

When I think back, I think we were amongst the first victims of
the free gift marketers. First of all, it was the absolute bits of
tat that they gave away free in comics. One such was a piece of
over-hyped trash grandly called 'The Thunder Clap' which was given
away in a comic called The Topper. So, what was this powerful-
sounding piece of equipment? Was it some kind of explosive device
or a small nuclear bomb? No, it was two triangles of cardboard
about eight inches in length that had another triangle of paper
glued along the edges inside it. When you held one corner and
wafted it through the air, the triangle of paper was forced
outwards by the air pressure, making not a thunderclap but a
rather ineffectual 'POP'. This didn't stop me doing everything I
could to buy this comic. Running errands, rounding up pop bottles
to return, anything I could. Sadly, I was too late, and they had
sold out when I had gathered up the required funds. I was
inconsolable. Dad asked me what I was sulking about and I told
him. My friend Graham showed him his own Thunder Clap, and Dad
just rolled his eyes. 'Come back in half an hour' he said and then
disappeared. When he returned, he was carrying something about the
size of a coffee table. He had made me his version of the
aforesaid Thunder Clap, but mine was about two feet long and
contained industrial strength brown paper inside it. It almost
made you sprain your wrist when you wielded it. It was like a
claymore. The effort was worth it though. It didn't make a POP,
but a quite pleasing THWOPPP. On the side of it, in felt tip
marker pen, he had written the words 'The Big Banger'. Quite the
marketeer my old Dad was! Added to the crap we clamoured after in
comics were all the choking hazards that they put inside cereal
packets (yes, in those days they actually put them in the package
amongst the cereal). For example, I had no end of small, plastic
soldiers. I had a shoebox full of them, but I wanted the free one.
The one buried elbow deep in Corn Flakes. Mam would say 'But, you
don't like Corn Flakes'. Was she crazy? Didn't she realise that I
didn't want to eat the buggers? The rest of the family could eat
those. To my surprise, she came home with a box of them. 'Does
anyone like corn flakes?' She asked the family. Dad said that he
would rather eat scabs, and my two sisters detested the things
too. I had sodding corn flakes for breakfast for about a month.
Still, it didn't cure me. I fell for it again when they gave away
a little piece of plastic that looked like a submarine. You put
baking soda in a little receptacle, and it (supposedly) would sink
down into the water and bob back up again when the baking soda
started fizzing. This would repeat over and over until the fuel
was exhausted. Problem one - I didn't know anyone who had any
baking soda, but Mam said that Steradent tablets would probably
work. After breaking off a piece and jamming it into the
receptacle, I dropped him into a sink filled with water. He just
dropped like a stone and haemorrhaged bubbles at the bottom of the
sink. 'How wonderful. More sodding corn flakes' I mumbled to
myself. Another free gift that springs to mind (probably in a
comic again) was something called something like The Whizzer. It

was a circle of cardboard with two small holes close together near the centre. Through these holes were threaded two pieces of elasticated cotton. When you wound the circle of cardboard up until the elastic had tightened, you pulled both sides, and it would propel it around. Again, Dad sprang to my rescue. He had taken the jagged lid of a baked beans tin and punched two holes through it with a nail. My Whizzer didn't just whizz. You could amputate a finger with it. As I have probably said previously, we weren't a particularly wealthy family, but on TV they advertised a pair of children's shoes. They were called Wayfinder shoes. Instead of having the regular tread pattern underneath of wobbly lines, these had animal tracks on them instead. Also, contained inside a compartment in the heel, under a little flap, was a minuscule compass. I gave Mam all the usual stuff, like 'But all the kids at school are wearing them. You really hate me don't you?' to which she replied 'No, I will always love you, it's just now, and then I wish I had never married and had kids. Harsh but fair on reflection. Needless to say, I never got a pair. To think, these shoes may have saved my life. If I was lost out there in the wilderness and I saw animal tracks, I could merely remove my shoe and compare the animal tracks. I could then trudge through the mud of the wilderness wearing one shoe and a woolly sock on my other foot following my trusty compass due north until I reached the nearest native settlement. Now I am older and wiser I don't fall for these things any more - do I? It is said that the only difference between men and boys is how much their toys cost. I am in danger of eBay inviting me to their Christmas do, I buy so much stuff on there. Usually musical instruments, antiques and fishing tackle. Perhaps if I could find an antique fishing rod that played tunes, I would find my nirvana. Speaking of fishing, I purchased a scarf type thing called a Shemagh or Keffiyeh. It is a square of checked material about a yard square. The idea is that you first place it over your head as would a lady with a headscarf, but then you wind it across your neck and your face until only your eyes are showing. Yes....those things that terrorists wear. I was informed, in no uncertain terms by my better half, that I was NOT to venture outside wearing it as she had to own me. It's hanging up behind the door. I did secretly buy an Ushanka though and hide it away in my fishing tackle box. It is one of those big, furry Russian hats with the flaps that you can drop down, so they cover your ears. Just the job when pike fishing. Mine even has the hammer and sickle on it. I look like part of the Red Army fishing team. I have absolutely no doubt that my gin-fuelled gullibility will stay with me until my dying day. You will know when I pass away. Just look for a strange dip in the price of eBay's shares.

The 1960s - A Breath of Fresh Air

Sometimes I miss the old two up, two down terraced house I was born in - I was actually born in it. Upstairs in the front bedroom. It was No 5 in a row of twelve. It was a community in the real sense. Everyone knew and helped everyone else. We had open backyards with no separating walls, which contributed to further foster the community feel to it. It was no unusual thing to find your neighbour had brought in your washing if you were out and it had started to rain. Similarly, they would put a spadeful of coal on the fire for you if you were out to keep the fire in for you on cold days.

For the first twelve years of my life, I thought the whole world was like this. A path of around ten yards or so led to a toilet at the bottom of the yard. The toilet door opened outwards and had no lock on it. It also had a three-inch gap at the bottom of it. This was pre toilet roll days. There was a supply of small squares of a newspaper that hung from a nail on the toilet door. I remember the arrival of our first toilet roll, and mother's warning of 'Don't go using it, that's only for guests'. So, we had an ornamental toilet roll to show people that we were going up in the world. I remember Dad saying 'It's for wiping your backside on, woman. It's not headed notepaper'. He then grabbed the toilet roll and his newspaper and headed off.

That outside toilet had much charm about it. Especially at night when you had to go there armed with dad's cycle lamp for illumination. I remember one November night when I had just settled myself upon the porcelain when a rat ran underneath the door, closely followed by a cat. The two of them ran around the walls like a wall of death before finally bolting back out underneath the door. One could say that I very nearly shit myself, but that was the whole purpose of the visit.

I don't know what it was about sitting on the toilet and being able to hear the sparrows chirping and feeling a breeze blowing around my ankles from the gap under the door that made me feel good, but somehow it did. It felt natural and right - somehow healthier. There was none of the 'I would give that five minutes if I were you' problems. It was almost like being in the open, and any unpleasant odours dissipated in seconds. On a breezy day, instantly!

If someone was occupying the toilet, I could walk a few yards and use Nanna's, who lived four doors down. Winter brought its problems though. If you suspected a heavy frost, you had to put a paraffin heater in there to keep the pipes from freezing. A paraffin lamp was often enough. It kept the temperature just above freezing point. Also, there was no light in there, so you had to take a torch. Either that or just take aim and hope!

Our toilet was quite roomy. I don't know what it had been before being a flush toilet. There was enough room in there to hang a big tin bath from a sturdy hook on the wall. This gave me a plan. I had been outside in the backyard one dark winter's evening when I popped my head around the door and told Mam I was going round to Nanna's house. What I actually did was sneak inside the toilet and hid behind the big tin bath and waited. After about fifteen minutes I heard the sound of feet on the cinder pathway and heard the latch on the door click and saw the door open and close through the crack between the bath and the wall. I heard a cough and recognised it as my cousin's. I waited until she was settled and heard the tinkling water sound and I let out a long, mournful wailing noise and started banging the sides of the bath. She screamed like someone about to be murdered, and I heard the door being flung open. By the light of the moon, I could see the streak of pee leaning from the toilet to our back door. I was utterly helpless with laughter and quite literally rolling around on the floor. Dad came flying out of the back door holding a poker and ready to do battle when he saw me and laughed. 'It's only our David buggering about' he announced to the anxiously waiting family. Everyone found it hilarious (apart from my cousin of course). Stupidly, I tried this trick again a couple of weeks later, but this time (and unluckily for me) it was Dad. He heard me let out the wail, and the next thing I knew the bath had been jammed hard against the wall by Dad's foot. He then proceeded to bang nine bells out of the sides of the tub before slinging the bath with me in it through the toilet door. Dazed and crawling out of the tub I saw Dad standing and the toilet door. He said 'Let me have a pee in peace you little bugger', then he slammed the door behind himself.

I also remember it being a place where my sister went to have a crafty ciggie. Even though Mam and Dad knew she smoked, it was something you just didn't do in front of them - even though they both smoked themselves.

Another game I devised involved clambering on to the roof of the toilet to wait in ambush. It was easy to do. You climbed onto the bin and then the adjoining wall and on to the roof. There was a gap at the top of the toilet door just wide enough to fit the muzzle of a water pistol through it. I picked my targets carefully though. If I saw it was Mam or Dad, I didn't do anything.

I remember one bonfire night. Our houses had a small piece of waste ground behind them, and then there were the backs of the newer council houses and their backyards. I had let all my fireworks off early, and I heard the people in the council house back to back with us come out to light theirs. I climbed onto the toilet roof and had a ringside seat to their far superior fireworks party. Speaking of fireworks, I once remember my cousin waiting until my dad was settled in there with his newspaper before throwing a banger beneath the door. BOOM..the noise was spectacular. There then issued forth a string of screams and expletives, closely followed by dire warnings about what would happen once he emerged. It was such a fortuitous shot, as the lit firework had landed right inside his underpants and trousers that sat at his feet, thus writing off a pair of his Y fronts.

The house was fairly basic with all the hot water coming from a small gas boiler on the kitchen wall, no bath and an outside toilet, but so what! It was where my world was. All our wonderful neighbours and the kids in my little gang.

When I was eleven, we moved into a council house a mile away, and they pulled down our beloved little home. It felt like we had moved to Mars. No one knew anyone around them except maybe the next door neighbours. It took a few years to readjust.

Now, the bathroom looks like a perfume counter. We have an extractor fan in there to stop the smell of excrement drifting casually down the stairs. Times are different. I agree, I no longer have the backyard safari with a torch in sub-zero conditions to relieve myself at one o'clock in the morning, but I think something beautiful has been lost to the world. It doesn't feel like an occasion any more. I suppose it is only now that people are beginning to use that word 'community', and talk of building one in their neighbourhoods. To us, it was the most natural thing in the world. In fact, the alternative seemed like madness!

Everyday Magic

We lose many things between childhood and adulthood. One of the saddest losses is our sense of magic. I'm not talking about some chap in a suit asking you to pick a card. I'm talking about the real magic. The tangible, touchable magic. It flowed through my veins. I was willing to believe in so many things. Father Christmas, The Tooth Fairy, Jack Frost and some other unsavoury characters like Ginny Green Teeth who dragged children into the lake to their death.

The world held wonderment and joy. Dad could ward off all monsters and Mam could cuddle and kiss anything better. I remember being told by one of my friends that Father Christmas didn't arrive at all. It was all just a story. It was only your parents putting your presents at the foot of your bed. That was the beginning of the death of the magic inside me. It almost felt like a bereavement. A small fragment of something wonderful had fluttered away like a sweet wrapper in a cold, December wind. The world became a little more ordinary and dreary.

Ghosts were real though and still are as far as I am concerned. You would think that they would have terrified me. One actually did, but most were only there as I was drifting off to sleep. They had always sort of been there. Commonplace other-worldly beings. There was the strange, smiling young man who would stand in front of my wardrobe. He would then wink, and walk backwards into the wardrobe. Right through the door as if it wasn't there. It was as if he was just absorbed into it. There was also one who I felt. I felt the weight on the corner of my bed as if someone was sitting there. Both these anomalies felt almost comforting. The one that did scare me was a time when I had been ill. My legs were like jelly. I stood at the top of the stairs and shouted down that I wanted something to drink. The only light on the stairs came from my bedside lamp in my room, I could see maybe three or four steps downwards, and the rest was in darkness. I then saw a woman sauntering up the stairs. I didn't recognise her. I thought it might be a neighbour or one of Mam's friends who had come to attend to me. As she neared the top of the stairs, the goosebumps ran up and down my spine. I said to her 'I can see through your legs'. I let out an ear-piercing scream and threw myself between my bed and the wall. When my mother reached me, she told me when I was much older, that she had never seen such terror on anyone's face. She said that my lips were blue and my face was ashen white.

I would read books in bed, even when I wasn't supposed to. I would hide a book and my torch underneath my pillow, only to sneak them out and read by torchlight. It gave the books a kind of other-worldliness. Yes, again that word, magic. Reading them by torchlight and seeing the gorgeous illustrations. There was just the page illuminated like a film screen, and beyond that, only the blackness of the room. I was blessed with so little, as were all my friends. But I was blessed with a strong sense of whimsy and a powerful imagination. I think my mother knew that I did this illicit reading, but ignored it. She must have figured that at least I was reading, so it had to be educational!

I also felt nature and the change of the seasons very strongly. It was as if I was 'hard-wired' to feel them. A little like the same gut feelings that the birds get when breeding season arrives, or when it is time to leave for warmer shores. Each season had its own delights. The fields and hills, the ponds, lakes and woods were my playgrounds. I was never bored. We band of happy kids could always find something to do. A den and a fire always seemed to occur. A prevalent theme. Boys and a campfire go together like any pair of things you care to name. Romeo and Juliet, Edward and Mrs Simpson, Marks and Spencer. A fire was a primal force. It made us feel slightly more grown up. Boys also had the ideal equipment to extinguish such flames too. We had our own mini fire hydrants. The hiss of the embers and the pleasing plumes of steam as the streams of urine hit it was a source of great fun.

We made rope swings in the trees, looked for puffball fungi in the woods and squeezed them to see the plume of fine, smoke-like spores emerging from the top, like smoke from a dragon's egg. We also went fishing in the ponds, lakes and mill lodges. We were trained and adept at making fun out of what was around us. We needed very little in the way of equipment. Just what we already had. Our wits and imagination. In many ways, when spring, summer and autumn were around, we were almost feral. Only returning for meals.

I do not miss my childhood. Not as such. Everyone has to grow up. It's how the world is. My childhood was cut short due to the illness of my father when I was around ten years old. It became basic, financial survival after that. That is probably why all my childhood memories are so fresh and vivid in my mind. They have become distilled due to their foreshortening. It was as if a chapter had been abruptly ended and all the memories and fun had been packed away and stored in an old shoebox under the bed.

The 1960s - Lancashire Dialect

There are so many quirky sayings that I have heard so often that I no longer question them. I come from a small, North West mining and weaving town named Leigh. My birth certificate says Leigh, Lancashire, but the boundaries commission found that far too complicated, so they simplified it to Leigh, Wigan Metropolitan Borough, Greater Manchester - far simpler. It kind of falls off the tongue doesn't it?

It seems that everywhere in the world you would ask for fish and chips. The fish comes before the chips, being the main ingredient. We always said 'Chips and fish'. I still do occasionally, if I am in a hurry.

My mother was the font of many quirky bits of language. One of her favourites was 'I'll go up Leigh now, then I can get back'. We all knew what she meant. It wasn't such a rough area that a curfew had been set and you might not be able to walk the streets after a certain hour. She merely meant that if she went now, she could get back in time to do other things.

Certain words were also altered. For instance, pneumonia was often pronounced as 'Pew-monia'. I knew one older work colleague who pronounced certificate as 'Sustificate' and compromise as 'Com-promise'. Pronounced as two separate words of 'com' and 'promise'. I remember him telling me once that 'The doctor gave me a sustificate, but it weren't right, so personnel had to come to a com-promise over it'.

Another word that was often used as a substitute for the correct word was the word 'called'. It was used as a substitute for the word 'supposed'. For instance, you might say 'I was supposed to be meeting her tonight, but I have changed my mind'. This would likely become 'I was called goin' out wi' her tonight, but I cawn't be arsed'.

A splendid and very versatile word is 'Eyup'. This can mean many things, such as 'Excuse me, you are in the way'. This would become 'Eyup, shift yerself'. It can also be used as an exclamation of surprise. Where you would usually say 'Hello, I wonder who this is?' This would likely become 'Eyup. Who's yon mon?' It can also be used as a word for impending trouble, as in the well-known phrase 'Eyup father, there's trouble at t'mill'. One of the best uses is as a greeting when you haven't seen someone in a long time. This would be something like 'Eyup! I've not seen thee fer ages'.

Another phrase that is used locally is Barm Cake. These are soft buns, teacakes in some places, even oven bottom muffins. But in Leigh, they are invariably Barm Cakes. Barm was the yeast left over after the beer brewing process. Rather than waste it, many bakeries used it as the yeast in their bread baking. Thus was born the Barm Cake. As an apprentice learning my trade at the local Technical College, a 'chip barm' from the refectory was more-or-less my staple diet.

The pot used to collect the barm from the brewery was, of course, a barmpot. This also became an insult, as in barmpot. Meaning a crazy or foolish person. Many of our words come from Norse words. One such derivation being the word 'Gormless'. Originally, Gaum (as it was spelt in the old Norse way) meant mindful or cautious. Therefore gaumless became gormless. Gorm meaning mindful - and less meaning less. So if someone is gormless, they are a little bit 'away with the fairies' and not paying close attention.

Someone with a squint would be referred to as 'a skenner'. As in 'Look at you mon. He skens like a bag o' whelks'. There is even a pub that is colloquially known as 'Skenning Bob's'. One can only imagine that a former owner had a very noticeable squint.

Numb was a word used more often to mean stupid, rather than an area of flesh that had lost feeling. A favourite phrase of my Dad's was 'He's as numb as a petty board'. Meaning that he was as numb/unfeeling as a toilet seat. Dad had many wondrous insults for stupidity, such as 'If your brains were made of gunpowder and it went off, there wouldn't be enough there to part your hair'. Or 'He is as dim as a Toc-H lamp'. Google it. It would take too long to explain. Their logo is an oil lamp. Also, for penny-pinching, mean people, he would say 'He's as tight as a bullfighter's britches'.

People no longer use such colourful insults. They resort to the quicker, four-letter equivalent. I think many of these old retorts were a work of art. They lent a certain air of gravitas to the insult. It became a tailored option rather than the off-the-peg four-letter equivalent.

Cack-handed can also be used in two different ways. It can mean either clumsy or left handed. Somewhat of an insult to left-handed people, but remember, these were the days when many children were forced to write with their right hand.

Our teachers had our own best interests at heart I suppose, but they were never going to get us to enunciate correctly (or speyk proper as we would say). We would try and speak the Queen's English, but we would invariably put 'H's where there were none. As in 'Yes mother, I would love a hard-boiled 'heg' for breakfast.

Thankfully, regional accents are now being seen as something to treasure. They are comforting, homely and honest (or 'omely and 'onest as we would say). They are part of our identity and speak down through the generations. No doubt many Lancashire accents were heard on the Plains of Waterloo, and no doubt before. It was the tongue of our fathers and mothers. It was our badge of pride and identity. It was ours, and we loved it.

My Answer

My teacher always told me
that I wouldn't amount to much
Said all that silly Lancashire talk
is only Double Dutch.
If you enunciate properly
you will get a better job.
You will earn more wages.
Take home a few more bob.
Now won't that be so worth it?
No dialect - you see?
Well I'd rayther still talk Lancashire
If it means turnin' out like THEE

My Mate Fancies You

During my early teens, girls were a mysterious and alternative breed to us boys. One day they were playing alongside us, building dens and riding bikes, and suddenly they started to grow breasts and turn into women. Before you correct me and say that they weren't actually women, but young girls. I am fully aware of this, but in truth, they all acted like they were twenty years old. They began to talk about such things as relationships (although this was a term that wasn't really used back then. It was just who was going out with who). Also, around this time, a sort of time-slip occurred. Girls of our own age were no longer interested in us, but now wanted boyfriends one or two years older. A sixteen-year-old boy stood a bugger-all chance of interesting a gorgeous sixteen-year-old girl. She wanted eighteen-year-old Gary, 'Because he has a job and a motorbike'. God, how I hated these boys. Sat astride their phallic symbol motorcycles while talking to these simpering, chuckling girls. You would think butter wouldn't melt in their mouth to hear them speak to Gary and his kind, but they could verbally cut you to shreds if you even dared to say hello.

I can remember the very moment when I kissed a girl properly for the first time. I was around 14 years old, and it was the last day before we broke up for Christmas. Our form teacher had allowed us to have a sort of impromptu party in our form room. The school record player was borrowed, and everyone had brought in records. All the girls were dancing, and all the boys were sitting around nonchalantly as if dancing was some kind of high, homosexual pursuit. One of the girls suggested that we played 'Spin The Bottle'. For anyone who has never heard of this game, a great deal of fun can be had with an empty pop bottle. The idea is that everyone sits around in a ring on the floor in a 'boy girl boy girl' format. The bottle is placed flat upon the floor and is spun around. If it is a boy who spins the bottle, whichever girl the bottle's neck pointed to when it came to a standstill, he had to kiss. A girl stood up and gave the bottle a good spin. To my absolute alarm, it pointed at me. I was now in totally uncharted territory. I stood up like a condemned man and advanced towards her. The next thing I was aware of was her pulling me in towards her. I just stood there with my arms by my side. In truth, I had no idea where to put my hands safely. She then planted a soft, lingering kiss upon my lips. I felt as if my legs had turned to jelly and a certain tingle began in a particular area of my body. The kiss can only have been for two to three seconds, but in that short space of time, she had turned me into a semi-comatose grinning idiot. I was brought back down to earth with a bump when all my classmates were shouting 'Come on, sit down, you've had your turn'.

As she sat down, she shot me an enigmatic smile and gave me a wink. I remember talking to my friend Ivan afterwards, and saying 'Hey, girls are great aren't they?' He said 'Yes, Dave. They are absolutely splendid'. I then asked him a question. I said 'Do you know when she just kissed me. Well, she slipped her tongue inside my mouth. It felt really nice. Do you think it was an accident?' He looked at me and sighed, then said 'We need to talk, Dave'. He then educated me on something that he called 'French Kissing'. I listened with a touch of amazement and disbelief, before saying 'She isn't French is she??' It seems I had an awful lot to learn, but I had been awoken to the joys of the opposite sex.

The other thing that boys lack around the age of sixteen is any form of sophistication. Girls were ranked on the 'totty' scale. The prettiest girl being referred to as 'Top Totty' and 'fit'. The word fit didn't mean athletic and in good physical condition. It meant sexually attractive. Boys were also consummate liars. We bragged about how many 'birds we had done'. If we had rounded up all these spurious numbers to the nearest round figure, the count would have been identical for all of us - zero!

We also acted like chimpanzees and performed pointless and dangerous stunts to try and impress the girls. I remember riding my racing bike past a wall with three girls sitting on it. To show my daring and the mastery of my machine I attempted to ride past them without holding the handlebars. The millisecond after I had shouted 'Top Totty' at them, my front wheel hit the kerb, and I went full length on the tarmac. It is fair to say that I have never heard girls laugh so much, so raucously and for so long in my entire life. Between sobs of laughter, I heard them say things like 'I can't breathe' and 'I think I will pee myself'. To add insult to injury, I had also buckled my wheel. When I tried to wheel it away, the front wheel looked like it belonged on a comedy circus bike. It also made noises like a rusty hamster's exercise wheel. This set them all off laughing again. The last words that I heard as I trundled off were 'What a tit'.

It is these small memories that add the tone to the otherwise drab watercolour of our past. Semi-painful memories, but for all that, they are tinged with gold. A person without anecdotes is a person who has never truly lived. I think our generation was the last to still retain a specific measure of innocence. There wasn't any internet, and even the girls in the 'mucky magazines' weren't fully nude - and if they were, they were turned sideways on so none of their bits were on show. I think the teens of today have things far tougher than we could ever imagine back then. They are bombarded from all sides by images of physical perfection that they are led to believe is the norm. I am happy with my era, thank you.

Folk Remedies

I have no idea whether it was some kind of aftermath from before
the NHS when people couldn't afford to see a doctor, but our
streets were steeped in folk remedies. People actually swore by
them. As a kid, I more often swore *AT* them instead. One such
remedy that springs to mind is putting slices of onions on the
soles of your feet and putting your socks on over the top of them.
It was a fiddly thing to do in the first place. You were then
supposed to sleep while wearing these stinking socks. They say
that it cured colds and flu. One thing is for sure, the smell of
the onions drifting up from beneath the bedclothes must have
helped to clear the sinuses.

Sometimes I was subjected to the 'Full Monty'. Onions in my socks
and Vicks vapour rub on my chest. The room was positively toxic.
What weirdo first discovered this supposed remedy, and what on
earth was he doing to accidentally find it? Now it is doing the
rounds on Twitter that putting Vick on the soles of your feet also
cures a cold.

Some of the remedies actually did work. Senokot was a brand name
of a senna based product. This was designed to cure constipation.
Or as my Grandma used to say 'It will put a road through you'.
Quite an effective description. As a child, It put a three-lane
motorway complete with lay-by through me! People back then seemed
fixated with bowel movements. They wanted to function like
clockwork. If a drastic remedy wasn't required, then a stick of
hard liquorice or a bowl of prunes seemed to do the trick. My
granddad ate treacle butties on brown bread every day and said he
never had any problems.

Then there was what may be called 'Preventative Medicine'. The
stuff we took to fend off illnesses. Thankfully, I was never
subjected to Cod Liver Oil. My sisters were though. I took Halibut
Oil capsules as a child. They were a liquid with a sort of gelatin
coating. I loved the taste of them and would pop the capsules with
my teeth. If allowed, I would have gone back for seconds. We also
got Orange Juice from the milkman.

We had other remedies such as Comfrey. A plant that grew on waste
ground near us. It was known locally as Knitbone. As the name
suggests, if the leaves were applied to a limb, they helped to
speed up healing. I never saw them used for that, but they did
seem to work on bruising. I still buy and use Comfrey Oil today.

My mother used to talk about such things as Bread Poultices and
Mustard Plasters. They sounded positively primitive. Mustard
Plasters were used to clear your chest of phlegm, and Bread
Poultices would draw out splinters. Apparently, they also worked
on boils. She also mentioned something about wearing a hot potato
somewhere or other. I can't clearly remember what for, but I do
remember rolling around in laughter when being told.

We were also told, as children, not to pick Dandelions as this made you wet the bed. The local nickname for them was piss-in-bed's. I think this is a case of a little knowledge being a dangerous thing. Dandelions have long been known as a diuretic and were used to cure kidney problems. They obviously put one and one together and came up with seven. Mind you, I have no doubt that the power of auto-suggestion occasionally made this happen, which further justified the legend.

Rhubarb was also used as a general 'blood tonic' (whatever that means) and was commonly grown. I remember as a child a neighbour of ours used to have massive stands of Rhubarb in his garden. These were large stems of the stuff. As kids, we would sneak under the bushes and steal a stalk from this virtual forest of Rhubarb. We would then go home for a paper bag and put some sugar in it. We would then dip the raw, unwashed Rhubarb into it and eat it. Delicious! All this came to an abrupt halt one morning when a friend and I were on our way to go fishing. We saw the old chap open his bedroom window and hurl the contents of his chamber pot all over the Rhubarb. No wonder it grew so well!

They told us all kinds of nonsense as kids. Things like 'If you pull a face and the wind changes, you will stick like that'. But the most stupid thing I was ever told was that if someone unscrewed my belly button, then my bottom would fall off. I dare say it was the same all over the country. Each area has its own set of local remedies and folklore. This is what makes this small set of islands such a vibrant place to live. The older, gentler ways are being swept aside on a tide of medical advancement and cynicism. Scratch beneath the surface though, and there is still a willingness to believe in 'the old ways'. As the magic disappears from our lives, it is filled with nothing to feed us spiritually. It may well be the placebo effect, but if it works, it works!

Clubland - The phenomenon of the 60s Working Men's Clubs

Most people will have seen Peter Kay's TV series Phoenix Nights. Although comical and somewhat exaggerated, he portrays the spirit of these establishments perfectly. A few years ago I had a discussion with some fellow musicians who are slightly older than me. They were musicians in a variety of pop bands who made good money touring the clubs after work and at the weekends playing cover versions of whatever was in the 'hit parade' that week. If you mention the phrase hit parade to today's generation, they have absolutely no idea what you are talking about. To us, it was on a par with the league tables in football.

One of them showed me his diary. Most weekends it was a Friday night booking, then on Saturday they would do a lunchtime spot somewhere, and on to another club for the evening. Sunday was just the same. They told me that they could have work every night of the week and twice at weekends and never go to the same club twice in a year, and all this within a ten-mile radius. They were absolutely everywhere. Clubland was thriving, and they were always packed. I only started playing around 1972, and even then, I was in a folk band, but the clubs were always looking for new acts, and us doing comedy Lancashire material, we got the odd gig.

It was a different world. We were used to playing in folk clubs in upstairs rooms in pubs. We found that in clubs we had a dressing room! On the dressing room walls were dozens of promotional postcards showing sequin-bedecked entertainers in unrealistic singing poses. Also many bands with exotic sounding names something like 'The Chicago Cougars', but when you looked at the contact phone number it was a Wigan number. I remember one concert secretary asking us where our stage gear was. When we told him that we were in it (Jeans and checked shirts) he just looked at us in wide-eyed wonderment. 'Well, I want you on for three, twenty-five minute spots, the last one being a dance spot' he said. When we told him that we didn't do a dance spot, his reply was 'You do now'.

We did the first spot after the bingo, then another session of bingo between the first and second spots, and of course another bingo session between that and our 'dance spot'. That dance spot was something that I will never forget. A dance floor full of couples desperately trying to dance to 'Gypsy Rover' and other such folk songs. Eventually, he took pity on us and brought the organist and drummer back on.

I remember several wedding receptions being held in these establishments in my early teens. It was in one such place, and at the tender age of thirteen, I had my first pint. My uncle asked me what I would like to drink, and I told him a lemonade. He looked at me and blinked a couple of times before saying 'No....what would you like to DRINK? The penny dropped. 'Oh, I'll have a pint please' I replied. 'That's good, now we are getting somewhere. A pint of what?' He asked. In a state of panic, I looked above the bar at the price list, and a word jumped out at me - Mild. 'I'll have a pint of Mild please' I said. To my way of thinking it sounded like the weakest and least damaging of all the drinks. After all, it was called Mild!

What looked like a small bucketful of dark coloured liquid was handed to me. I took a sip, and it tasted dreadful. 'Oooo that's lovely. I like a nice drop of Mild. This is what I always drink' I told my uncle (somewhat unconvincingly). It took me most of the evening to drink it. My uncle asked me if I wanted another, but Mam stepped in and said 'One is enough for him. I don't want him being sick all night'. It was also at a wedding reception when I would be about fifteen, I smoked my first Hamlet cigar. That time I really was sick!

Clubland was pretty much all there was for entertainment in the North West for the adults. As teenagers, we had the all-nighter at Wigan Casino, the home of Northern Soul. I found it all a bit too much. I danced appallingly. Someone once asked my friend if I was some kind of special needs case. Well actually, he used far less politically correct terminology, but it amounted to the same thing. I only went two or three times. By then the folk music was taking over.

Clubland carried on until the late seventies, but they were dropping like flies. Some carried on and diversified, hiring out their halls as venues for parties and wedding receptions. Later they became places for Slimming World, Line Dancing and craft fairs. Very few are left now. A lot are now 'Venues'. Either restaurants or nightclubs.

It was an era that passed by without any fanfare or sad goodbyes. They just faded away and into history. Town centre pubs began to fill up, or people stayed at home to watch their colour TV's and brought in a few beers from the off-licence. They were places where the concert secretary was a god. He usually had his own microphone to make any announcements whenever the fancy took him. I once remember one Elvis impersonator on stage. He was right in the middle of his big number. He was singing 'American trilogy'. He was down on one knee and putting every ounce of emotion he had into the words. He was up to the part where he was singing, 'I wish I was in the land of cotton. Old times there are not forgotten' He was just about to sing 'Look away, look away' when the concert secretary interrupted with 'There's a car causing an obstruction on the car park. The registration is....'. The Elvis impersonator shouted a rude word down the microphone and walked off stage, never to return. The concert secretary said 'Ee, he's a bit touchy isn't he?' to the assembled audience.

They weren't palaces of highbrow entertainment and culture. They were honest. People went there for a drink, a game of bingo and a

laugh. The entertainment was just the icing on the cake. I miss
them.

1962 - The Local Park

We sprang forth from our mother's bellies and into this world. We were as unwanted as weeds upon a building site by society in general, but we were loved. Dressed in hand-me-downs and laughter. Unfettered by the slow and tarnished wisdom of unbelieving adults, we were millionaires in the currency of imagination. We were six or seven, but we had it all sussed out.

The local park was Disneyland for free. Our friends were the raucous and waddling mallards upon the lake that laughed outrageously. They competed for the bread that we threw. Later, they were seen bobbing along on the surface of the glinting mirror-like lake, like motorboats.

There were the swings, the banana boats, the spider's web, the lethal and tooth-chipping rocking horse, the sand-pit and of course, the slide. We would find pieces of discarded bread wrappers that were a sort of waxed paper. We would rub it upon the metal of the slide and polish it with the seat of our trousers to a perilous shine. One lady sent her toddler up the steps, while confidently assuring him that 'Mummy will catch you at the bottom'. He shot past her while screaming like a wayward express train. He did a 'Barnes Wallace' bounce, before coming to rest six feet past the end of the slide in a bawling furore of tears and snot. I don't think I had witnessed anything quite as funny in all my tender years. I believe she called us 'Hooligans and guttersnipes'. Far from being insulted, we felt quite honoured to have such a grandiose title bestowed upon us.

Near to the park was a little off-licence, we would pop in and say 'Mi Dad wants five Woodbines and a penny book of matches'. I'm pretty sure that he knew the father was completely fictitious, but if he didn't sell them to us, then someone else would. Once the contraband had been obtained, we would slip behind the Rhododendron bushes and 'spark up'. The Woodbine would be passed around like a joint. We had all been instructed to smoke with dry lips, but someone would always forget, and the cigarette would be passed on with a wet and flattened end. 'Ewwww, you've made a ducks arse of it' the unfortunate recipient would complain.

I think I was elected the brains of our little gang because I was the one with the weirdest and most twisted imagination. This fact was proven correct in a most achingly embarrassing way in the very same park. In our gang were two brothers. Twins, but not identical twins. We were all in the park and accompanied by their grandma. She was on a park bench several yards away while we fed the ducks on the park lake. One of the twins (Let's call him Neil, to save the real person any embarrassment)announced that he needed the toilet. We all told him to pop behind the bushes and have a wee. He said 'No, I want the toilet - properly'. To this day I have no idea why such an awful idea popped into my head, but I said, 'Why don't you do it in that litter bin? We will all stand around you, so no one sees you. He replied that he had no intention of doing any such thing - until I said the magic words. 'Why, are you frightened?' 'No, I'm NOT. Ok, all stand round me and turn your backs'. He said. Then he dropped his shorts and hoisted his buttocks onto the edge of the litter bin.

As soon as we heard him 'mid-dump', we all ran away laughing. Now, in my mind, this was entirely sufficient, but his brother ran across to his grandmother and said 'Look, Nanna, our kid's having a poo in a litter bin'. I laughed so much I couldn't breathe. That same evening, his grandma knocked on our door and told Mam the entire story. I only heard snatches of the conversation, but one memorable sentence was 'So our David told your Neil to have a jobby in a litter bin, and HE DID?' She nodded in agreement. I heard my mother guffaw with laughter. She said 'None too bright is he?' and closed the door. My mother said to me 'It's times like these I remember just why I love you. You will either be rich or go to prison'. To date, I have managed neither.

John Logie Baird Has a Lot to Answer For.

I suppose I was one of the first generations to be born into a time never to know life without television. I was born in 1955, and my parents bought a TV to watch the Queen's coronation in 1953. The first set that I remember only had a twelve-inch screen - and that is measured diagonally from corner to corner and not widthways. For some reason, it resided in the kitchen in our old two-up, two-down, in an alcove beside the fireplace (Yes, we had a coal fire in the kitchen).

The 'telly' was prone to going on the blink and had been the recipient of many a thump on top to put it right again. It also had a tendency for the picture to scroll, and Dad had to fiddle about at the back of it to find the horizontal hold knob.

One day we were watching 'Wagon Train' when the picture began to get smaller and smaller. Fortunately, it was almost at the end of the programme. We all gathered closer and closer to the set, desperate to see how the programme finished. Eventually, the picture was no bigger than a postage stamp, and we all jockeyed for position with our noses just inches from the screen. Eventually, it made a 'Pop', and the picture disappeared entirely. The telly repairman was called for, but he proclaimed the patient 'dead on arrival'. 'The tube has blown. It would be dearer to fix it than what it's worth - and that's assuming you can still buy the tube' he told Dad.

It was decided that we would rent a new set. The new set was bigger, and we all agreed that it should be in the front room. Unlike our old bakelite set, it had a lovely wooden surround, and Mam liked the mahogany effect. She put a round, lace-work doily on top of it to stop the little pottery dog ornament from scratching it. Thus our home entertainment system was installed.

We had become a family that viewed together. I believe we have all become a little spoiled with modern technology, and therefore we don't truly value what we have. I not only have a full HD TV with satellite but also Now TV and Amazon Fire Stick. I can pause and rewind live TV and watch whatever programme I like whenever I like. With internet access, I can also download more or less any film ever made. Even with all this I still whine on and say 'God, there's bugger all on'.

When I think back to the couch and both chairs of our cottage suite being filled to capacity with bottoms, and only two channels to watch, but yet we felt like millionaires with our new telly, it just doesn't remotely compare to today. Eventually, BBC2 came along, and Dad was in his element because he could now watch live, floodlit, Rugby League, all commentated upon by the inimitable Eddie Waring.

It was the early sixties when the influence of American TV

programmes began to be felt. Most of the programmes were imported. A whole plethora of Westerns. The aforementioned Wagon Train, Bonanza, Rawhide, The High Chaparral, The Rifleman and many more. I also remember Batman coming along, starring Adam West and Burt Ward. I also remember this being the start of merchandising. I remember being given a cheap, chocolate Easter Egg perched on top of a pottery Batman mug. The whole ensemble was wrapped in that crackly cellophane. After all, nothing says more about Easter and the resurrection of the saviour better than a Batman mug. He got out of a life and death scrape every week! Bizarre though it was, no one ever questioned it.

In my teens, the telly also gave me Top Of The Pops, and later, The Old Grey Whistle Test. Both essential viewing for any self-respecting spotty teen. Pop music, in all its forms, was the currency of conversation on the streets, and it also brought us into contact with that exotic species, the girls, when we went to the local disco.

I suppose television came into its own during the seventies when colour arrived on the scene, and those with a few bob could afford a colour set. We had to wait until around 1980 before we got ours. It was mesmerising. We would have watched anything because it was in colour - and we did! We watched everything from The Galloping Gourmet to What The Papers Say. Stuff we wouldn't have even looked at in black and white. Dad was also have been in his element because Rugby was now in colour. Sadly he passed in 1971.

We criticise the kids of today for being glued to the telly, their phones and their laptops. When you consider what we had and what they have now, I think we would have been no different. Let's think - shall I kick a plastic football around in the street with my mates in any weather, or shall I play a video game in HD full colour in the warmth of my centrally heated bedroom? Hmmm......tough call.

I do honestly believe that people are people and we all take the path of least resistance to our pleasure, and kids even more so. I think television in itself and the whole family sitting around it for a nights entertainment is on its way out. People are beginning to watch what they want and when they want to watch, on whatever device they choose. Be that a small television set in a bedroom or office, through to computers, tablets and smartphones. We are slowly losing the sense of community that we once had when everyone was squashed together on the sofa and remarking on what was on. From Dad telling my sisters to 'turn down that rubbish' when The Beatles were on telly, to him telling everyone to be quiet while he watched the rugby, or checked his football pools results.

An era has passed, and the worlds global village has become smaller and smaller, yet perversely we have all become hermits inside our little technological bubble. The only time we ever truly live is when there's a power cut, and we all learn the lost art of conversation by candlelight.

I miss the Radio Times and the arguments about who watches what. I miss the camaraderie of the living room and the banter. I miss the Christmas specials of Morecambe and Wise and The Two Ronnies. I suppose I miss my Mam and Dad and when we were a family. I think, in short, I miss my youth. I have lived a life defined by the milestones of television. The assassination of JFK, England winning the World Cup and the moon landings. All this laid out in front of my young and impressionable eyes. Take me back there, please. I don't like it here any more.

Fishing in the Mill Lodge

We were nine or ten years old, and most times we could be found by Tunnicliffe's lodges, fishing rods to hand. We were fishing for anything that would bite. With floats made from porcupine quills and our baskets to sit upon, we were content with the world. That's all we needed. A little pot of maggots for bait, a handful of floats and hooks, a bottle of water to drink and a few sandwiches. That was us set for the day.

I suppose our main quarry was the obliging and greedy little perch. His hard, scaly exterior with alternating dark and light stripes, and a spiky dorsal fin to prick the fingers of the unwary. Once you caught one perch, the chances were that there would be several more. We never caught the exotic stuff like carp. It was mostly roach and perch, but also the gudgeon. These fish came along in massive shoals. The bed of the lodge would turn black with them. You could catch two or three, one after the other, without changing the maggot. They are beautiful, streamlined, iridescent fish. They are only small things, the record weighing in at around four ounces, but what they lack in size they make up for in character. They fight well for their size too!

We would chat all day about every topic under the sun. Laughter and teasing each other about things was a large part of the day. We would see the occasional large carp leap clear of the surface before landing with a spectacular splash, which would send small tidal wave ripples that made our little floats dance on the surface. This was the biggest thrill of all. The elusive and almost ghost-like old man of the lake. His power thrilled us. We almost feared doing battle with this awesome wizard.

Although the mill lodge was a finite and brick enclosed water, our imaginations at what lay beneath its surface both excited and intrigued us. When that float shot beneath the water, there could be anything on the end of the line. There lay the thrill. It is almost like putting your hand into a hole and knowing there are creatures on the other side. It is primal and dark in some ways but gives so much pleasure. This feeling has never left me. Although I am now much older and wiser to the ways of fish and expect to do battle with the old man of the lake, I still get that same primal rush when the float goes under, and I strike and assess the size of the fish on the end of the line. Occasionally you think you have hit a snag, and the hook is stuck somewhere – but then it begins to move, and for the first time you feel the awe of its strength and power.

Big fish are not stupid. They know every inch of their domain. They know the thick patches of weed and the submerged tree roots, and their only present purpose is to take you there. It becomes, to them, the macabre dance of life. You can but do battle and use your skill and wit to win the day. When these big boys finally succumb and slip over the lip of the landing net, it is almost a small anti-climax. They are no longer wizards. Their myth has become real. Then care and concern set in. To gently land these magnificent beasts, remove the hook from their lip and carefully put them back into their kingdom.

Every large fish I catch, I look into his eye and make contact. My soul and his (or hers of course). The next big thrill is to see the tail pulse in the water and the ponderous, dark shape slip back into the night of his domain.

On return home, I am greeted with 'Did you have a nice day?' I always reply in the same way. I say 'Yes it was great'. Only another fisher-person would truly understand. Only another who is touched by its magic would understand the way that the rod buckled with the majesty of natures fury. I have had people say to me 'But you don't eat them, you just put them back'. I smile and let them have their moment. They have absolutely no idea of the feast that they provided. The banquet for the soul. The hearty and wholesome meal for the mind, and the piquant dessert course of seeing these magnificent beasts swim free again, secure in the knowledge that I and others like me have concern for their welfare and secure their futures with our hard earned money. Without us, their worlds would likely not exist.

The old saying goes 'Give a man a fish, and you feed him for a day. Teach a man to fish, and you feed him for life'. I would also like to add 'Teach a man to fish, and you turn him into a lover of nature'. When my friend Graham spoke those six words to me 'Would you like to go fishing?' Little did he realise that he had changed my life forever. God bless you mate!!!

Teenage Parties 1960s and 70s

If you Google the word 'Party', this is what it says:
Noun: a social gathering of guests, typically involving eating, drinking, and entertainment.
Verb: enjoy oneself at a party or other lively gathering, typically with drinking and music.
Indeed, some of the parties I have attended have been like this. Other parties haven't even ticked one of the above boxes. These parties are usually the ones thrown by the parents of a teenager on their birthday.

The primary duty of parents is to encourage and help their child to grow and develop into a well-balanced adult. Many parents have a strange idea of what their kids find cool. They even use that phrase too. Such words as 'cool' when your parents say it, sounds about as natural as John Boy Walton saying 'Yo bitch'. I can assure them that inviting a Punch and Judy man to the party of a thirteen-year-old boy doesn't fall into the category of cool. I have never felt greater pity for anyone in my entire life. He sat there cross-legged on the floor with the rest of us with a 'kill me now' expression on his face. His parents were primary school teachers. I do not offer this up as an excuse. They should have been prosecuted for child cruelty. They did provide a splendid buffet of sausage rolls, triangular-cut salmon paste sandwiches, and a trifle made in a bowl about the size of a baby bath, so all wasn't lost.

Parents shouldn't be involved in teenage parties when the recipients are over the age of fifteen. They should hire a room somewhere with wipe-clean walls. Set up a trestle table with paper plates, plastic cups and an enormous amount of cakes and junk food, then also supply a decent, loud record player. They will sneak in their own booze and take liberties with each other's bodies as they do anyway when you aren't watching. This didn't happen though in the late sixties to early seventies. We had to be chaperoned.

I remember a friend of mine whose parents were more trusting and allowed their seventeen-year-old son the run of the house when they went away for a weekend. A party was swiftly planned. A REAL party. The concept is blindingly simple. He had a record player, so everyone brought some records and bought bottles of booze that they were woefully unprepared either mentally or physically to drink. There was a healthy mix of the sexes. This meant that there was one girl for every three boys, thus making the girls even more unattainable (though many of them became startlingly attainable after half a bottle of Woodpecker cider). Add to this a few cigarettes with contents that didn't come from a tobacconist, the emotionally unstable hormones of teenagers, and hey presto. You have a 'Waco' type scenario in the making.

Things started warming up when a friend of mine whose name I will withhold (his father was a police officer) went up to the bathroom, stripped naked apart from a pair of shoes and socks, came downstairs and went for two circuits of the council estate where the party was. The neighbours of the boy whose house it was happened to be walking home from the Labour Club when they witnessed his activities. He responded by waving his genitals at them (the streaker, not the boy whose house it was). By this time I couldn't breathe properly I was laughing that hard.

At this party, one of the guests - a girl, brought with her a make-up bag of epic proportions. Some drunken party animal decided that we should all have our faces painted like Bowie (David Bowie, the pop star, not Jim Bowie, the American frontiersman and inventor of a particularly lethal knife). I remember having the Bowie lightning stripe down the middle of my face. Instead of Bowie's back-combed auburn hair, I had long hair with a centre parting, a bit like Neil out of The Young Ones. It wasn't a good look with the face paint. I looked like a satanic Jesus.

I remember the bathroom being in constant use, for either the effect of copious urination that drinking alcohol provides or the type of projectile vomiting that it also brings. The queue was about eight deep on the stairs, and a heard a girls voice saying 'Are you alright in there Julie? Don't cry. He isn't worth it. Have you got your asthma inhaler with you?' I thought that this might be a long job, so I went out through the kitchen door, through the backyard gate and proceeded to urinate against the wall. Having come from a brightly lit kitchen into the pitch darkness made me temporarily unable to see too well in the dark. Unbeknown to me there was a courting couple only two feet away, and it was a breezy alleyway, which meant I had been urinating down his jeans leg. I beat a hasty retreat.

The party ended when another neighbour, a rather large gentleman with tattoos who was a long-distance lorry driver, hammered on the door and told us that the party was to end immediately. A friend of mine named Michael made the mistake of saying 'Go on then, make us'. The lorry driver grabbed him by the collar of his Afghan coat and slung him through the garden hedges. Two days later, I heard through the grapevine that all the neighbours said that they had witnessed a naked, drunken orgy. An orgy?? I didn't even get so much as a snog. The result wasn't all bad. He instantly became a teenage legend. We still laugh about it to this day.

Under a Summer Sky - More Tales Under Canvas.

'Look...up there. Those stars that look like they make the shape of a saucepan. Do you see them? That's 'The Plough' that is' I said. It was late July, and Graham and I were stretched out on our backs on a blanket and staring up at the skies. We were both about twelve. You couldn't have scripted it better when a shooting star flew across the sky. 'Make a wish', Graham said, 'But don't say what it is, or it won't come true'. It must have been somewhere around midnight. We were camping out on 'The Point'. A finger of land that jutted out into the lake (or Flash as it is known - after flash flooding due to mining subsidence).

We had set up camp around 5 pm and had a happy little camp-fire going and our tent next to it. A green, waxed cotton two-man affair. The classic 'Baden Powell type, with no groundsheet. We didn't need it. The grass, the moss and the leaf litter felt like a feather bed. The blanket would serve as our groundsheet. The camp-fire threw eerie, dancing shadows against the tree trunks and bushes. Beyond the range of the fire, we could see very little, until we turned our backs to it. There wasn't a breath of wind, and the reflection of the moon sat upon the water like a big, golden beach ball. A fish leapt clear of the water, and the ripples made the moon dance a little quadrille on the surface. The crest of each ripple throwing off a silver twinkle. I little realised it at the time, but that was probably the purest, earthiest piece of magic I had ever witnessed. We could have been anywhere. As it happened, we were a mile from a council estate.

We had brought along our mugs, plates, spoons knives and forks, plus all our provisions. I partially filled a saucepan with water and balanced it upon the embers of the fire. Soon it was boiling. I poured it into the waiting cups, and we had our first brew. We felt like men. The tea had the vaguest hint of wood-smoke about it. Many years later I tried a cup of Lapsang Souchong for the very first time, and its smoky flavour propelled me right back to that exact moment. We watched the embers die away, and both of us noticed a chill descending. You could hear every tiny sound with amazing clarity. We listened to the happy sound of someone wobbling home from the pub and singing 'I'll Take You Home Again Kathleen' (and not very professionally). This was followed shortly after by his voice and his accompanying female mingling together in laughter and merriment. We both knew it was time to climb inside our impromptu sleeping bags - two tatty old eiderdowns. One each. Together with a cushion each that we had borrowed from our respective sofas.

Graham switched on his pocket transistor radio, and we listened to the static as he tuned it in to a channel. We accidentally stumbled across a black sounding American voice. He was playing music from records that he called 'Da Blues'. It was the first time either of us had ever heard it.

We both decided to tell each other ghost stories. Perhaps not the wisest choice of material, as soon we were both thoroughly creeped out. It was a little later we heard a shrill, piercing scream. We were petrified. Then it happened again. 'Somebody's bein' done in' I said. Neither of us knew that it was a fox. What made us do it, I don't know, but we scrambled around inside the tent for our knives and forks. We felt a little more secure then. I don't know what we thought we were going to do with them. Eat the attacker?

Neither of us got a wink of sleep until we saw the sun begin to peep over the horizon. Only then did we feel safe, and we zonked out. We finally rose sometime after eight. We scrabbled about to find some dry grasses and twigs and lit another fire. We made two cups of tea, and then put the beans into the pan after throwing out the excess water that was left over. We had baked beans for breakfast. Slightly cold in places, but wonderful.

It was time to fish. I remember watching my float one moment, then the next thing I woke up as I hit the ground. I had fallen asleep. We were both shattered. We de-camped and headed off on the short journey home. The idea was that we were both going to go back that same evening, but once in front of the telly on a Saturday night, that was us done for the weekend. It was the first of many trips, and still, in my eyes, the very best.

I remember the later years I spent under canvas. We needed no clock, for the sunlight streaming in through the tent walls was alarm enough. Waking to the sunshine and birdsong, then the realisation of where I was would dawn on me. Still sleepy-eyed I would then go back to sleep for another hour or so. Soon, the sun would make the tent stuffy and unbearable, so it was time to face the day. Priorities - light the primus stove and put the kettle on. Pour some cornflakes into a bowl and pour on the milk. Once on the other side of a hot brew from a tin mug that burnt your lips and a bowl of cornflakes with tepid, slightly on the turn, sun-warmed milk, it was time for the day's adventures.

One such trip was on the Isle of Anglesey on a campsite close to Eilian Bay. Depending on the tides, you could fish off the rocks, and within minutes catch half a dozen mackerel for lunch. Mackerel that fresh is a million miles away from the fresh fish in the shops. It is light, sweet and fragrant. It hasn't yet developed that oily quality. A few fillets sizzling in a frying pan in a little Welsh butter when only forty minutes earlier they had come out of the sea. It has to be experienced. The taste defies description. I happened to be camped by a hedgerow, and in the field beyond was a wild growth of Meadowsweet. The smell of the frying Mackerel, the salt tang of the sea and the vanilla overtones of the Meadowsweet all combined into a heady bouquet. To add to the medley of sensations, I could hear the lonely piping of Curlews in the distance. Fresh air and well-cooked food compliment each other so readily and only serve to heighten the experience. The tea always tasted so much better outdoors too.

After lunch, I would take out my sketchbook and pencils and head off to do some drawings. There is a lovely little church there called The Church of St Eilian in Llaneilian. It has some fabulous carvings, and above the rood screen is a painting of a skeleton, with the motto 'The sting of sin is death' (or something remarkably similar). I spent many a happy hour sketching within the peace and tranquillity of that gorgeous, old church.

I remember many sunny days, but also several wet ones. There's something hypnotic about the sound of rain hitting the canvas. Especially at night. The gentle lullaby of the raindrops. One unfortunate year I had a tent with a sewn-in groundsheet. A good idea in principle, as long as the tent didn't leak - and mine did. As my friend remarked 'Do you want to sleep in the deep end or the shallow end tonight?' We arranged a makeshift flysheet out of builders polythene to keep out the rain. One old seasoned camper remarked that it wasn't quite the done thing. 'Well, you sleep in a sodding puddle then, and we will book in at a B&B' my friend replied. Wherever you go and whatever you do, there's always an expert. The reason you know that is because they can't help but tell you!

We used to do quite a lot of sea fishing on holiday. Either spinning off the rocks for mackerel or beachcasting for the cod and ling. We also used to go down to Bull Bay at low tide and check the rock crevices for crabs. Only selecting those of a decent size and ignoring the smaller ones. It was the freshest of fresh crab. I still know how to cook and dress a crab.

There were also a couple of pubs that we knew who turned a blind eye to us only being sixteen. We would go and play darts and sip at our pints. One landlord would stop our tap at two pints though. 'I don't want you technicolour yawning all over my bogs - you've had enough' he would say. We were hardly in a position to argue. We would pick up a bag of chips each from the village and head homewards. I remember pottering the three miles or so back to the campsite by the light of a pathetic torch. Every time we would swear that in the morning we would buy a better flashlight. We never did. My friend likened the light that it gave off as being like a radish in a stocking. I had to agree.

Once back at the tent we would light the Tilley Lamp. That lovely hiss it gave off, and the yellowish light. Once lit, everything outside and beyond the lamp's light was just inky blackness. It's only when you are camping that you smell the grass and the trees.

All senses heightened. The sound seems to travel for miles. I once remember being asleep when we heard something shuffling about behind the tent, issuing forth little grunts and noises. 'What's that?' my friend asked. 'How the eff do I know? Who do you think I am, Doris Stokes?' I replied. (She was a well-known medium at the time). We thought it might be a wild boar (not that there were any around there). With some trepidation, and by the light of our pathetic torch, we ventured outside clad in nothing but our underpants. It turned out to be an inquisitive hedgehog who could probably smell the bottle of milk in our tent.

I always slept well under canvas. The fresh air was almost like a general anaesthetic. I was asleep in no time. The dawn would start to illuminate the tent at about 4 am. I would squint at my watch and say 'Sod that' and go back to sleep. Some of my happiest times have been spent under canvas, either on my own or with a gang of us.

When sunrays were the clothes we wore
and rain our sweet salvation.
When silent homage to the earth
was a whispered dedication.
The youth that through our veins did coarse.
It brought our souls together.
Those memories so cherished still
will fuel my soul forever.
When my time is here at last,
if heaven it is real.
It will look like Anglesey
That's how it used to feel.

Wigan Road - Coming Full Circle

The mind is a marvellous thing. It bathes the memory in a warm,
sepia tone tint. It levels out the wrinkles and bumps, leaving
just the shiny, beautiful grain of the memory, like a well
polished, loved and hand worn piece of wood. It leaves the patina
of the memory shining through.

My small world seemed boundless in its mystery and appeal. From
the 'tanner rush' at the pictures on a Saturday morning, where we
saw the cartoons and short clips like The Lone Ranger, to the
cigarette smoke and jostling mackintosh crowd of the rugby match.
Within sight of the ground were my school and the Parsonage
Colliery headgear and chimney. Overlooking the ground was the mill
of J and J Hayes. As a child I was always asked if they were
relatives - sadly they weren't.

While at the rugby match we would buy a scalding hot cup of tea in
a flimsy plastic cup and a penny lolly from the cafe under the
big, wooden scoreboard. You had to hold the cup gingerly by the
rim until it cooled down sufficiently to hold. We would dunk our
lollies into the tea and suck at the melting sugar.

That was my town. The land that bred and moulded me. The red
brick, cobblestoned, streets were like something from a Lowry
painting. The slum clearances had started, leaving the shells of
once loved family homes. They now lay sad, empty and windowless.
They were our adventure playgrounds. Scratched into the paintwork
of one of the door surrounds were marks, with inscriptions like
'Alfie - aged six, 1953'. The touching progress of a child's
height, inscribed with love, into a door frame. No doubt they
thought this would be forever. There were other names there too,
but they have slipped this old memory.

Everyone seemed to smoke back then. Whenever we took the bus, we
would always clamber up the stairs to try and get the front seat
on the bus. The smell of stale cigarette smoke and the leatherette
seats. It said above the window 'Please do not spit on the floor'
Someone had scratched off some of the letters, so it read 'Fleas
do not sit on the loo'.

The blue and cream Leigh Corporation buses with a conductor that
took no cheek and doled out tickets in an efficient but humourless
manner. I wore those horrendous, round clinic specs that fastened
with a sort of spring arrangement behind the ears. They wouldn't
have come off in a plane crash. They were quite literally strapped
to your face. Consequently, I gained the nickname The Milky Bar
Kid.

Everything in those days was buttoned up. None of your casual
open-collared shirt. Even the top button was fastened. I also
tucked my jumper inside my pants. Perhaps some kind of sign of
insecurity. I have no idea. I must have cut quite a comedic figure

in my tucked-in jumper and clinic specs. I must have looked like a surreal, working-class owl.

Angels, we were not. We occasionally smoked, spat, fought and were rebellious. Anywhere that mischief came calling, you found the usual suspects. The punishment was immediate and non-negotiable. I remember my Mam slapping my legs as she held on to my arm, while I ran round in circles trying to avoid her. I was then sent to bed with red hand marks on my legs, and all because I pulled my tongue out at Mrs Tyrer. When I compare that to today, the difference is startling. I am making no comment as to which approach was right. I am just noting the difference.

School was generally unpleasant and thuggish, and something to be endured rather than enjoyed. I do not deny my childhood and my more than humble roots. That said, poverty is not a badge of honour. It is more like a baptism. The mark of the struggle is tattooed upon your heart. You are never left untouched by those lessons.

Save the string, that carrier bag might come in handy, that coffee jar will do to keep my wood screws in. I even have a baked bean tin that has been meticulously washed out and any sharp edges eradicated where the lid once was. It sits on my desk right now as I am typing this. It holds my pens and pencils.

I suppose that's why my imagination developed and grew. It was an escape from a less than ideal childhood. Poverty has a stigma that can't be hidden. It shines like a beacon from the recycled clothing that we wore and the mended and patched jeans, way before such things were fashionable. My first bike was basic, to say the least. It had been cobbled together from bits and pieces by an uncle. No unnecessary luxuries were needed - such as brakes. I got proficient at putting the sole of my shoe against the front tyre. It rarely worked, and I have emerged through to the other side of many a privet hedge.

Many toys were cobbled together from what lay around, and sticks became swords or guns. We made fun with anything. Collecting old cans and using them as target practice, or dribbling them noisily down the street like a football. I wouldn't swap one second of my childhood. Even the horrendous bits. We made do with what little we had. We were appreciative of the simplest things. Even to this very day, I like people to buy me bits of useless, cheap and quirky crap for Christmas. After all, who doesn't need a pencil sharpener that plays 'Una Paloma Blanca'?

Life is a hand at cards. Some you drop and others you pick up. One day the game will end, and the pile of winnings you have made will be useless to you. 'No pockets in shrouds' as my Gran used to say (amongst other things). It reminds me of lines from a Simon and Garfunkel track on 'Bookends'. 'Time it was, and what a time it, it was. A time of innocence. A time of confidences. Long ago, it must be. I have a photograph. Preserve your memories. They're all that's left you.'

The Old Farmhouse

An old house is more than a building. It is a testament to life and a vessel of memories. Anyone who has scraped through several layers of wallpaper and down to the stippled walls beneath will know about the arduous journey involved.

I live in an old farmhouse. I remember having to remove some old plastering on the walls in one of the bedrooms. It contained pieces of hair. This was used to give strength to the plaster and help it to bind. At first, I thought it was some kind of animal hair - that's until I found a perfect curl of brown hair. There was no mistaking the fact that it was human. The builders had obviously been round to the local barbers and swept up the hair from the floor to use. Perhaps they had some kind of deal with the barber? Who knows? All I know is that it felt extraordinary to be holding the hair from someone who probably died maybe a hundred and fifty years ago.

The original part of the house is made from hand-made brick, and the mortar used was probably the traditional lime mortar. Again, this often contained clay and other materials. The whole wall was basically local and in a way, organic. Is it then such a long stretch of the imagination to believe that in some way an old house can 'remember' things? I know that it was during renovations that odd things began to happen. The first thing to be heard was the footsteps. We would be downstairs watching television when we would listen to the floorboards above the ceiling creak. This would then be followed by a series of foot-falls walking across the room, from the bedroom door towards the window when it would cease. A few minutes later the journey would be reversed. Was this someone worriedly walking towards the bedroom window to look out over the fields for a loved one? For anyone who believes in ghosts, then no proof is necessary. For anyone who doesn't believe in ghosts, then no evidence is possible. I always look for a reasonable and rational solution, but sometimes I come up empty.

The most exciting thing is the walking man. You catch him (I just assume it's male) out of the corner of your eye. He enters the room through where a door used to be but is now a small window. He then walks along, turns right into the hallway and disappears. If you turn to get a look, you see nothing. I put all this down to imagination until one day the dog happened to be lying at my feet as the shadow entered the room. The dog perked up his ears and watched the shadow follow the same path that I saw from my peripheral vision. One day I decided to set up a digital voice recorder. I left it on the sideboard where the shadow walks past. I took the dog for a walk, so the house was completely empty. I recorded the distinct sound of two steps from someone wearing a pair of clogs and walking on a stone floor. He then stopped and turned on the spot. You hear a sort of sliding sound. The entire floor is carpeted, but beneath the carpets is a layer of concrete, and beneath that is stone flags.

The bedroom that was refurbished had a desk in it that held my PC. I am now going back to Windows 95 days. I had a floppy disc (no, I didn't need to take tablets for it) that held a couple of important letters. I left it beside the keyboard and went downstairs to make a cup of tea. When I returned, the disc was nowhere to be found. I assumed it had accidentally slid beneath the PC box, so I lifted it up and placed it on the floor. I then proceeded to take absolutely everything off the desk surface. I decided then to give it a wipe over with a cloth to remove the dust. I checked the floor and the litter bin but didn't find it. I then put everything back onto the desk. I got it into my head that I must have absent-mindedly taken it downstairs with me when I went to make a brew. I went back down to the kitchen to check, but it wasn't there. When I went back upstairs, the disc was back in exactly the same place that it had been initially.

Things got even weirder. I had come home from work and had the house entirely to myself. The front door is more-or-less permanently locked as we just use the back door. I unlocked the back door then closed and locked it again behind myself. I then walked into the downstairs toilet and sat down. A few seconds later I heard a male voice right outside the toilet door say the words 'By heck, it's cold out there today' and then a laugh. I struggled to get my trousers back up in my hurry. I came out of the door like a greyhound out of the traps saying 'Hello? Hello?' The voice was so loud and pronounced, I was convinced I had an intruder. All the door and windows were locked. I searched that house from top to bottom. I even looked under beds and in wardrobes. I found nothing.

Later that year we had family round for Christmas. We were all in the living room when we heard a scream. One of the ladies had been sitting in the toilet when someone whispered the words 'Ruth? Ruth?' directly into her ear. She came flying out of the bathroom, almost tripping over in her haste to exit. She was in a right state. Oddly enough, years later when we checked through old census records of 1911, there was a servant who lived in the house with the family. Her name was Ruth.

There were lots of other things that happened, including the footsteps of someone running along the roof. It is a pitched roof and has slates. It would be impossible to run along, but the steps were so loud and booming that they made the windows rattle. We also had a spate of internal doors being bolted. In the end, I took all the old bolts off them. I'm glad to say that things have quietened down considerably. I can't remember the last time anything happened.

A friend of mine loaned me a set of metal dowsing rods (don't ask, it's a long story). I tried them out in the house, and they swing inwards at a certain point on the floor. This seems to run through three rooms, all in the same place. I have had other people try this without telling them where the spot is. It happens to them too, in the same spot. Maybe it's a ley line. Perhaps it's an underground stream. Maybe it's just a coincidence, I have no idea. I only know it happens every time I try it. The only thing I can say is that I have never personally felt threatened or scared by anything. My other half had when I was out one night, and she was in bed, and the dog kept running up to the bedroom wall and growling ferociously and barking. It would then scoot backwards in fear with its tail between its legs. The whole process would be repeated over and over. This went on for about 20 minutes I am told. Maybe it is haunted, perhaps it's a case of the Stone Tapes theory when the fabric of the house can absorb and record events and play them back like a video recorder. Maybe it's all my imagination, and I am losing my marbles? Who knows?

Sweet Hope

There is always hope.
Often it hides in the cracks.
It slides behind the cushions
like an errant coin in a sofa.
Hope is the cup of tea
after words and many tears.
Hope is when you wake again
and greet the daylight with relief.
Hope is the glue
that keeps us all together.
Hope is the hand offered
from an unexpected quarter.
Hope is finding out
that you have touched a soul.
Hope is not a wish.
A wish is the journey
that hope may take,
lit by the candle
of a shining dream.
Hope is always there
though sometimes elusive.
Hope will never leave you
as long as you leave some room.
Hope is the greatest gift
that you can give to someone
and the cruellest thing
when taken away.
Love is the child of hope.
Love was baptised
at the font of tears.
Hope is brave and resilient.
Hope is the light
in the darkness of ignorance.
Never lose hope
It is so difficult to find again.

A Finer Vintage

The randomness of kindness falls
as honeyed words from those red lips,
and all around this mind and heart
the thoughts and deeds of yesterday
stir softly in my heart.

Those eyes have witnessed so much pain
yet gentleness in there abides.
Those trusting eyes and ready smile
framed by those lips of ecstasy
bring joy to my tired eyes.

If we could keep and bottle time
and drink once more these luscious days.
When life is so unkind and cruel
this beverage we now enjoy
would keep us ever young.

Life is wanton, wasteful, short
and these few moments of pure gold
are all that we can keep and hold
to fight against those frost-filled nights
and warm our wearied bones.

So I will raise this glass to you
remembering each second spent
with arms entwined and bodies close
when youth did course through every vein
and hearts did beat as one.

Who Ate All The Pies?

Well, I am getting hungry
it's only half past three.
So I am just a wondering
what shall I have for mi tea?
I have to go out shopping.
I need a bottle of gin,
and I've just thrown an empty box
of cornflakes in the bin.
I fancy a black pudding
and sausages as well.
Sod the sodding diet
yes, sod it all to hell.
I'll get some eggs and fry them
and bacon, cooked all crispy,
and half a dozen barm cakes
for dipping, soft and whispy.
Now, I'm feeling in the mood
I refuse to be a fake
If I'm doin' this proper
I'll have a sodding cake.
and beer, I must have beer.
Brown ale it is the best.
So I can sit there burping
with egg all down mi vest.
Then I'll hide the evidence
put the bottles in the bin
It'll be my little secret
Can you tell she isn't in?

My House is Haunted

Ghosts they are peculiar things
They're people that are dead,
and now their spirits wander past
when you're lying in your bed.
Some live in the closet
and some they walk the landing.
Why on earth they bother
it takes some understanding.
If I was dead I wouldn't waste
my time in strangers rooms.
I'd be more theatrical
and wail and moan in tombs.
Or be a phantom hitch-hiker
and flag down passing cars.
Or be a merry poltergeist
Throw glasses round in bars.
Walking on the landing
is such a waste of time.
But then you have the time to waste
which must feel quite sublime.
Yes, ghosts they are peculiar things.
They're people that are dead.
But I only want to go to sleep
when lying in my bed.

To An Old Friend

Come find me again
when daylight burns away
your eyes to red
and all your dreams
lie twisted and broken
by the slow and sorrowed
time you have known.
Come find me.

Come find me again.
I will be there somewhere
waiting to be the friend
that helps you lift
Each small and painful piece
and without thought
will mend your broken dreams.
Come find me.

Come find me again
and let my hands
repair your soul
and patch your wings.
To once again
take flight and soar.
Refreshed and fixed.
Come find me.

I will be here.
I will always be here.
This is a truth.
Think not of me
and fly again.
Until you fall.
Then come to me.
Come find me.

Childhood Friends

For I have known you
oh so long.
When we were only
six or seven.
You smiled at me
and I smiled back
and then you held my hand.
Such a thrill
to find a friend .
Girls aren't silly
like I thought.
I like your hair
It shines like gold .
Oh I don't understand.
I am just a boy right here,
and you are just a girl
but when we play
we laugh so much
and when we're scared
we cry.

The Lover

If all the stars they shine again
and planets turn and do align.
Then all the wishes in this heart
will melt and form these words so few,
'You own me, heart and soul'.

For I have glanced into those eyes,
and depths beyond the firmament
are there within those very eyes.
In that abyss I tumbled, lost
and never to return.

In your hands I place my heart.
For I am done, and lost in thrall
to all those pleasures and those pains
that beat within my heart so sore
that only you can soothe.

If I was but a humble dog
so very old and facing death.
With my last breath, in heart and soul,
I would drag myself to you
to die there at your feet.

My words seem shallow when compared
to all the wonderment I see.
You are the banquet of my soul.
I'm there in famine and in feast.
My love it knows no bounds.

I Went to Wigan Casino You Know!

I dance how I dance
and I dance just like me.
Don't look over here
there's nothing to see.
Just some old bloke
playing soul far too loud.
I bloody well live here
and so, I'm allowed.
No bugger's watching
You see, no one cares.
If you piss me off
well, I'll dig out mi flares.
I dance on the carpet
it gives a good grip.
If I dance on the lino
I'll put out mi hip.
Hip, there's a word.
I was in my youth.
But the girls never saw it
if I'm telling the truth.
I was always too shy.
I danced like a fool.
I looked epileptic
but thought I looked cool.
But now I don't care.
In pyjamas I dress.
There are no fit birds
that I have to impress.
So let me dance on
I'm the soul-man supreme.
I'm just an old fart.
I'll soon run out of steam.

Hairy Gary

Gary is a werewolf
but you won't hear him growl.
He sits and looks up at the moon
and gives a little howl.
He really is a gentle soul.
His kindness never stopping.
He sees old ladies across the road
and helps them with their shopping.
Gary is in training.
He goes there twice a week.
He's the world's first werewolf guide dog.
He really is unique.
So, put away your silver bullets.
No one wants him dead.
Give his little head a stroke
and kiss his nose instead.

Tea

When solace is so very rare.
When everything seems so unfair.
When no one really seems to care.
Brew a pot of tea.

When your mind is just too wired.
When you're feeling really tired.
When your heart in woe is mired.
Brew a pot of tea.

When none is wheat and all is chaff.
When you can't even raise a laugh.
Run yourself a good hot bath.
then brew a pot of tea.

Go and put your jim-jams on.
Then next, your dressing gown you don.
When your 'get up', it has all gone.
Brew a pot of tea.

Life isn't always wine and song.
Shit hits the fan and things go wrong.
One thing will help your mood along.
Brew a pot of tea.

When in heaven I am due,
and when St Peter comes in view,
He'll say 'We've been expecting you.
God's brewed a pot of tea'.

Reg the Vegetarian Vampire

I like a bit of mange tout
and a crunchy carrot or two.
It a shame I can't eat garlic,
but it makes me want to poo.
I'm having these strange feelings.
I'm struggling like heck.
You know I can't eat meat my dear
but I want to bite your neck.
I've tried to compensate you know,
sunk my fangs into a beet.
But all I want is your white neck
and I crave for the taste of meat.
I swish around in a temper
in my black satin cape.
I eat a bowl of couscous
and think about your nape.
My fangs a sinking into you
and blood just oozing out.
But you say 'Don't be bloody daft'
and slap my head about.
I never was a veggie
'til I fell in love with you.
You sit there with that smug face
while I am feeling blue.
Well smile now all you like dear.
both you and your daft brother.
You see, I got the last laugh.
I bit your sodding mother.

A Sacrifice to Change.

It was an old piano. I briefly thought about selling it, but no one seems to want them. This wasn't a particularly special piano. It was made around the 1920s I would guess, because of the Art Deco style engravings on it. There was only one thing to do with it - recycle as much as I could and dispose of the rest. It will live on though. I already have the beautiful mahogany put aside for projects. I now have boxes and boxes of wood screws, some cast iron, brass and lead to weigh in. It had a cumbersome iron frame inside it that took some shifting. Fastened down by large bolt type screws. This thing was built to last.

To allow access, I had to take my bolt crops and cut through the strings. It broke my heart. Each string that I cut seemed almost like a cry of pain. Each note rising higher the further along that I cut. I whispered the words 'I am so, so sorry' as I did it. Fran said 'I'm sorry. Did you say something?' I just shook my head and carried on.

It started me thinking about who its previous owners were. It was probably someone's pride and joy. Was it owned by some studious classical pianist? Or was it a good old family piano where some child went through the scales with a music teacher in close proximity, and at weekends, Mum or Dad would play songs, and everyone would sing? I imagine it played many carols in its lifetime. It started me reminiscing about Dad. He played the piano. It reminded me of when I was looking through family papers, and I found a handwritten note that was a receipt in my father's hand. It was an I.O.U. He had agreed to pay a relative in instalments for a piano. It was that same piano that Mam complained about many years later. She said she was always banging her elbows on it when she walked through the door, and with it being black, it always needed dusting.

One day, Dad and a neighbour manhandled it into the backyard and smashed it up with a sledgehammer. Mam asked him why he didn't sell it. His answer was 'It's my piano, and if I can't have it, it will break my heart to part with it and wonder where it was'. It was the first time I ever saw tears in Dad's eyes. It was like a family member was disappearing.

I remembered oh so many evenings with our front room packed with friends and neighbours. Dad was playing requests and everyone singing along. I also smiled when I remembered the voices of the ladies breaking up as they sang 'Nobody's Child'. Especially when it got to the line 'No Mummy's kisses and no Daddy's smiles. Nobody loves me. I'm nobody's child'. On such evenings I was allowed to stay up a little later. I would sit on the rug with a packet of crisps and a bottle of bitter lemon from the pub, alongside a couple of crates of beer for the assembled crowd. Little did I realise what pure gold this was, and how privileged I was to have witnessed this.

The house grew much quieter after that. It seemed to me that the house had somehow lost its beating heart. Dad had even stopped playing the piano at his local. It was almost like he was in mourning. Dad always wanted me to take up music, but I just wasn't interested. I remember him saying to me 'If you learn to play an instrument you will be taking up a hobby that will last you a lifetime. You will also be giving pleasure to other people'. He died when I was sixteen. It was shortly after that I started to learn guitar, before giving it up and moving onto fiddle and mandolin and joining a folk group. When I was twenty-four years old, I stood on the stage of the Free Trade Hall in Manchester in front of a full house for a charity concert. We were on with Mike Harding, Peter Skellern and the Grimethorpe Colliery Band. It ran through my mind how very proud Dad would have been. As I stood on stage I could almost feel his hand on my shoulder, and the words 'Good lad - proud of you'.

Music is a universal language. We sing songs of joy and sorrow. We dance to it and march off to war behind it. It speaks to us like nothing else and affects us like nothing else can. It was just an old piano, but I can still taste the dust inside my mouth from its demise. It was almost a living thing, but progress had dictated that its useful life had come to an end. We now want instant gratification. Click a button, and we have every song ever written at our fingertips. It is almost an obscenity. We want perfection without the struggle. Like fat cats, we lie back and say 'Please me'. The musician can be lonely in a crowd. He realises that if he is loved, it is because of what he does and not who he is.

Music is an obsession once it takes hold. It is something that is a road towards the same goal. The pursuit of excellence. When you play, and you get it just right, you can pick out someone in the audience and see the only thanks we ever need or crave. The tears in someone's eyes because you have moved them. It is moments like that for which we live.

Take me in your arms again
and let us dance without a care.
To feel your heartbeat next to mine
and bask in all the falling years
as once again we are sixteen
and happy to be loved.

Notes they fall and do caress
our hearts and souls, and with a kiss
I tell you just how much I care
You lean against me tenderly.
The world it seems to drift away
leaving but us two.

Soft notes from that piano fall
and as we shuffle side by side
You lean a little closer still
and on my shoulder place your head.
Your perfume and your loving warmth
fills me with desire.

No poem wrought with noble words
or flowery odes, no matter how
well crafted with such turn of phrase
can but compare in any way
to notes that drift and fall so soft
and make our bodies touch.

Music has such witchcraft, dear
and your bewitching eyes and smile
disarm me so completely now
that if the time we could roll back
You know, I wouldn't change a thing
For you are all I need

Online Nonsense

Bobbing along like a ball on a pond
or a stick in a fast flowing stream.
Drifting along as it all passes by.
The nonsense, and madness supreme.
Pictures and videos, words and strong views.
The trolls and the ones who don't care.
Though the message seems real and all above board
Before you press 'Share' have a care.
Truth is a concept, it's somebody's view
It's simply the way that they see.
Each view that you hold and share with the world,
there are many that just won't agree.
Oh, it doesn't say Easter on my chocolate egg.
You'll find that I don't give a jot.
Stop looking for things that just don't exist.
It isn't some terrorist plot.
When you track it all down and look at the facts
all the memes that you read are off whack.
They all seem to hold a small kernel of truth
but sadly the rest is all cack.

The Radiogram and Other Creations

It was only when I was much older and had to do bits of DIY around
my house that I realised just how talented Dad was. He had the
most basic of tools. A handsaw, a claw hammer, screwdrivers,
pincers, a bradawl, a wood plane, a hand drill (the old-fashioned
kind that you turned with a handle) and a tape measure. He did
everything around the house. Anything that needed fixing or making
he did it.

One day, Mam had arrived home and had been cooing over a radiogram
that she had seen in a shop window. It's not that she had an
extensive record collection. I think she owned three LP's in
total. Those were ones by Mario Lanza, Gerry and the Pacemakers,
and Perry Como (or Perry Coma as Dad called him). Dad asked why
she wanted a radiogram as we already had a record player and a
radio. Mam had no real answer, apart from saying that it would be
a beautiful piece of furniture. Mam asked for so very little, but
buying a new radiogram was a bit out of our reach. Even on the
'never never' as we called it. With three kids to feed and clothe,
there wasn't a lot of spare cash. Dad said 'leave it with me'.

A neighbour had an old set of drawers and a wardrobe that they
were going to put out for the bonfire. Dad asked if he could have
them. He then borrowed my uncle's shed and disappeared for a few
evenings after work. When Mam asked what he was up to, he told her
that he was helping his brother build a rabbit hutch. What he was
doing is making a radiogram.

He built the cabinet from the old wardrobe and set of drawers. He
sanded the wood back down to the rich mahogany patina and then
waxed it. It shone like a new conker. He later amalgamated our old
valve radio and record player into it. Where the speaker was, he
had made a fretwork sunray pattern. The only things he bought were
the backing cloth for the speaker grill, some glue, a handful of
nails and screws and the wax. He even did all the soldering
himself.

Mam came home after shopping to find the radiogram in situ. 'Oh
Seth, it's beautiful, but we can't afford it. It will have to go
back to where it came from' she said. When Dad told her that he
had made it from the radio, the record player and some old
furniture she didn't believe him. She started looking for some
label or other that said 'Grundig' or the like. It was only when
she dropped down the door to reveal the record player that she
recognised the record deck. I remember asking Dad why Mam was
crying. He said 'Because she is happy'. It made entirely no sense
at the time.

Mam invited all the neighbours round to see it. None of them could
believe that it wasn't shop bought. It was a gorgeous item. I have
no idea where it went. I can't remember it going, but it must
have. I know it didn't come with us when we moved to a council

house when they were demolishing our old house with the slum clearances. Maybe it was given to a relative. I would hate to think of it being smashed up.

Other things I remember of his was a bookshelf, a bedside table and a cactus stand that hung on the wall. The easiest way of describing it is that it looked like two interlocking squares. It never saw a cactus, but it did see quite a few of Mam's ornaments.

As a kid, he made me a pull-along train and carriages from spare bits of wood. Several guns and rifles etc, and a small bench for me to sit on in the garden. When I reached the age of ten, all this came to an abrupt halt when he had a stroke. He survived for another six years before passing. I have so very few things of Dad's. I have a few of his Buffs medals, a couple of wooden handled screwdrivers and his signet ring. I never remember him having small hands, but the ring won't even fit on my little finger. He was fifty-six years old when he passed. I still miss him to this day. He was also a talented pub-style piano player. I won't build him up by calling him a pianist, and I think he would agree with me. He was also a consummate wit and story-teller and a charming man. I honestly can't think of anyone who disliked him. I do wonder what he may have gone on to achieve had he been born into a more affluent society, but this is a semantic argument.

All my happiest memories of Dad are before his stroke, and these grow mistier day on day. Both my parents were cremated. They share a plaque on the wall around the garden of remembrance in Wigan cemetery. I rarely visit it, because I see no point. There is no actual grave. Perhaps this is a good thing. I have a very well developed sense of guilt, and not visiting their graves to put flowers there would be yet another thing to beat myself up about.

Talking To My Dog

I find myself talking to my dog quite a lot. He's a Border Collie,
so he is quite intelligent. He is three and a half years old but
seems entirely switched on to his wants and needs, and where he
fits in with ours. He wants feeding, clean water, somewhere to
sleep, regular exercise, cuddles and reassurance. It occurred to
me that he and I are no different in that respect. We are two
different life forms with one standard set of needs.

The fact that there are many things he can't do for himself, such
as earn a living, feed himself, brush himself and take himself for
walks doesn't lessen his value as part of our family unit. We love
him. He enriches our lives in ways too numerous to mention. He is
also loyal and would place himself between an attacker and us. In
short, even though he does not contribute to society in any
commercial or wealth-related way, he has a place.

Dogs also work for a living. His breed was engineered to round up
sheep. The fact that he doesn't do this, or thousands more like
him, doesn't mean that they are surplus to requirements and should
be put to sleep for the good of society. Over the past few months,
I have been examining some of the phrases that are in everyday
use. The aforementioned one being 'useful to society'. Just
because he doesn't contribute fiscally, or perform the task for
which he was bred, doesn't (in my eyes anyway) make him no longer
useful to society. He brings pleasure to people. Women coo over
him and stroke his head, and say such things as 'Oh, isn't he just
GORGEOUS'. I nod proudly in agreement, and secretly wish that they
said the same things about me.

He is also black and white in colour. If I were to look closely, I
would be hard pushed to see if he was more black than he was
white. Even if I did. Would it matter? Are a Black Labrador and a
Golden Labrador less or more useful in the eyes of society based
purely on what colour they are? You might say that I am ridiculous
for saying such a thing. People have said far sillier things, and
not about dogs, but people.

He is called Henry. We chose the name for no other reason than the
fact that we liked it. It sounded somehow rural and old-fashioned.
We didn't pick it because we are rampant royalists, and even if we
did, wouldn't this actually be seen as a slur upon our monarchy?
In fact, why give dogs a name in the first place, you may ask?
Again, it's because we wanted to. We can write his name on the
Christmas cards that we send to people. We see him as not just an
animal, but our extended family. We can shout HENRY, COME HERE and
he will come back to us. In short, we gave him a name because we
love him. There's that word again - love. We love him. He is no
use to the economy (apart from the fact that we buy dog food for
him which makes the pet food producers richer) but we wouldn't be
without him in a million years. Ask any good dog owner, and they
would agree with this.

It makes me wonder one thing. Why can't some of these people extend the same concept to members of their own species? It's down to the fundamental question. Define value to society and a person's worth within it. What are the parameters by which we, as a civilised society, measure this? Is it purely based on wealth? If that is so, then that is a society to which I do not wish to belong. I know of immensely wealthy people acting disgracefully and using their wealth to inflict catastrophic damage to the community, merely because of their need for more and more money.

I am aware of the fact that people are living on the streets who do not contribute financially to society, but neither do they currently take from it. They live by scavenging food from skips that have been thrown away by a wasteful society. We have the RSPCA, the PDSA, Blue Cross and several other animal charities - and rightly so. The sad eyes of a suffering dog seem to touch more deeply the heartstrings of some people than the sad eyes of a person sleeping rough.

Most people sleeping rough are not there through choice, or because they are lazy, or are drug addicts. They are there because they slipped through the net. I suppose this is why I prefer to talk to Henry. He neither agrees nor disagrees with me. He just accepts the situation and gets on with it. I, on the other hand, have no such excuse.

To Every Dog I have Known

I look into those soulful eyes.
It comes to me as no surprise
to see how much you trust.
My feeling they are laid quite bare.
To you, there's no one can compare
to me, it seems unjust.

You trust me so much it's untrue
and when my car pulls into view
you wag your tail like mad.
But all my duties I can't shirk.
I must go out to do my work.
You look so very sad.

I promise you 'I won't be long'.
I know you don't believe this song.
Then I am on my way.
While I'm sitting in my car
and driving off to places far
I think of you all day.

I take comfort, as I roam
with thoughts that soon I will be home
and soon my day will end.
It always thrills me to the core
when I open up the door
Who's waiting there? My friend.

Office Life - A Windy Day

Someone once said to me that there is nothing funny about
flatulence. I took issue with this and said 'Well it has its time
and its place!' He pressed me further to qualify the statement. I
told him that the failure to release flatulence is a dangerous
thing. I told him that I didn't advocate it in the middle of the
vicar's speech at a funeral, or during a Bach recital, but in the
privacy of one's home, it is a joyous thing. The louder, the
funnier. It was meant to be enjoyed. It is nature's little gift.

He mentioned that I lacked any form of social grace and that I
needed psychiatric help. I asked him how he dealt with his own
situation. He informed me that he would walk outside, and not
inflict it upon his family. 'So you walk outside, fart, then come
back in?' I asked him. He nodded prudishly in answer. 'What if you
have a curry, wouldn't they think you are on a sponsored walk,
with all that walking outside and back again?' I asked him. I
could see this had him flustered. I then played my trump card (pun
intended) 'What if you are on a train, or a plane?' I asked him.
By this time he had started to become a little agitated. 'You are
just picking extremes now' he said.

I hadn't asked for his opinion in the first place. A work
colleague had broken wind in the office, and I said 'More tea
vicar?' The farter and I both laughed. That was when he made the
remark. My colleague then started on him. He said to him 'Well
your arse is that tight, if you did fart, it would sound like
someone whistling for a taxi'. I found this both unexpected and
hilariously funny. He then threatened to report us to Health and
Safety. By this time I had tears rolling down my face. 'He's
reporting your arse as a health hazard' I said to my colleague
between sobs of laughter.

One of the girls asked what we were laughing at, and we told her.
'What him?' she said. I told her that it was indeed him. I also
told her that he walks outside to fart. 'So that's why he walks
into the corridor, stands for about five seconds, then walks back
in again'. This started me laughing all over again. I said to her
'Well that's another small mystery solved then eh?' The next thing
we saw is him leave his desk, walk into the corridor, then walk
back in again. 'Don't walk into the corridor. He's just dropped
one in there. You will bang your head on it'. My colleague
announced to the office, to great hilarity.

A few minutes later we received a message to go to the manager's
office. 'What's going on in there?' The manager asked us. 'I have
had (name withheld) come in here telling me you are all farting
like chimpanzees after a consignment of baked beans?', He said. We
told him it was just one fart, and that he had become all
sanctimonious about it. 'He walks into the corridor to fart. Did
he tell you that?' my colleague added. 'Does he now? Well, that
explains that funny smell. I've had them check the carpets for

damp twice' he told us. 'Some days it smells like someone has left the lid off a full dustbin on a hot day'. He went on to say.

We were sent back to our desks, and that was the end of the matter. A couple of days had passed. It was one lunchtime. The guy who didn't find any humour in flatus stood in the middle of the office, lifted one leg, and did a massive and very musical fart. 'Now what is in the least bit humorous about that?' He asked us. The whole room fell into hysterics. Janice, the chief typist, shouted at him 'You did that right in front of my desk you disgusting bastard'. By this time my stomach was hurting with laughter, and I could hardly breathe. 'Look around. Did that answer your question?' Janice asked him. He sheepishly sat down again. His face was beetroot red with embarrassment.

A day later a series of letters were delivered to every desk in the office. The letters read 'There is nothing funny about breaking wind. You must all stop forthwith' We were all up in arms until someone said 'Have you read the signature on the bottom of the letter?'. It was signed - Alf Hart.

We Do It 'Cos We Love It!

Ever since my early twenties, I have been a musician in a variety
of bands. One particular night, we had been booked to play in an
actual barn. Being a barn dance band, it was almost inevitable
really! The barn was used as a working barn. All its previous
contents had been moved out (in this case pallet loads of
potatoes) to leave a dance floor - of sorts.

There was a balcony some ten feet off the ground that contained
hay bales. Space had been cleared. This is where the band were to
play!! Leading up to this was an old ladder with one rung missing.
We decided to leave the P.A. Speakers at ground level and just
take our guitar amplifiers up there - which in itself was no
simple task!! Beneath this balcony (now filled with band members,
their instruments, and around two hundred bales of hay) they had
situated the makeshift kitchen. Health and safety obviously hadn't
thought this one through correctly! We were tuning up and doing a
sound check, and we all noticed a distinct smell of Calor Gas. A
few seconds later we heard a whoosh and someone scream, and a
split second later a ball of flame rolled past the front of our
balcony. There then ensued something like a comedy scene as four
lads all tried to get down a rickety ladder at the same time.
'Owwww get off my finger' one of the lads said as I put my size
twelves straight on it. 'Well move it, and I won't tread on it' I
replied. We all reached ground level safely, and the fireball had
been a one-off incident. The cooking range now seemed to be
working fine. We gingerly made our way back up to our erstwhile,
home-made, crematorium and began to play.

As I previously mentioned, this barn had been used to store
potatoes. Potatoes leave behind a very fine, dark grey dust, that
has the same consistency as talcum powder. The floor was about an
inch thick in this. As soon as the dancers started to dance, a
cloud began to form. We could only see the dancers from the waist
upwards. Small children had disappeared entirely! The dance was
brought to a stop while a solution was found. The answer was to
douse it liberally with water and then remove the residue with the
tractor bucket, spades and brushes. This left the whole barn
feeling cold and damp. It also made the floor a little treacherous
while it dried.

The interval arrived, and we made our way downstairs for the food.
Being a potato farm the food, quite naturally, was jacket potatoes
with either grated cheese or chilli - or both! We all plumped for
both. I don't know if anyone has tried eating a jacket potato on a
flimsy paper plate using a plastic knife and fork, but it is a
considerable skill, and one none of us possessed. This meant we
ended up wearing some of it.

During the interval they were selling raffle tickets, so we all
bought some. The second half started, and the dance floor had
dried and become a decent surface at last. Buoyed by alcohol and a

general atmosphere of Bonhomie, the dancers were loud and enthusiastic. It was a pleasure to play in such an atmosphere. It was at times like these when it ceased to become a paid job, and it became a pleasant pastime.

The occasion was someone's fiftieth birthday but was also a fundraiser for Cancer Research. She had been a survivor of this herself. She gave a very moving speech and told us all she felt so privileged to be here amongst all her loving friends. She was still wearing a scarf tied over her head to cover her bald head due to chemotherapy. It was an intensely moving moment. They then decided that this was a good time to mention that there were still raffle tickets for sale if anyone wanted them.

The dance resumed, and everyone was back in the groove and dancing enthusiastically. It came to the last dance, and we played the usual end-of-night song, which is Wonderful Tonight by Eric Clapton. The birthday girl and her husband danced in the middle of the dance floor. Quite a few were in tears. I had to concentrate on playing, or I might have been one of them. The dance ended and it was time to draw the raffle. We all sat there in expectation. I had bought about a fiver's worth of them. Prizes came and went, and then they announced the number of one of my tickets. I eagerly came forward with my winning ticket. Had I won a bottle of whisky, brandy, wine even? - No, I won a large sack of potatoes!!

Having a Curry

It had become a custom. Almost a crucial part of being part of our
band. After the gig, we went for a curry on the way home. This
involved visits to some establishments of a dubious nature. A few
spring to mind. One such was an Indian restaurant somewhere in
Cheshire.

The toilets were both sides of the foyer entrance. Leading to each
of the toilets was one step. It was somewhat dimly lit. In the
middle of the two sides was a smoked glass panel. I went to the
toilet. When I came out, I had forgotten about this step. I
stepped onto fresh air and went lurching forward. All in this
split second it ran through my mind 'Two more steps and I will be
fine'. I didn't have the luxury of those two steps. The smoked
glass panel was virtually invisible in the light. I hit it like a
rhino, forehead first at some force. It rang like a huge dinner
gong. I slid gracelessly to the floor. Even the staff, who were
helping me to my feet were laughing.

When I arrived back at the table, I couldn't see two of the lads.
On closer inspection, they were on the floor in convulsions of
laughter. I didn't see the humour in the situation at all. To add
insult to real injury, I had a big lump coming up on my forehead.
This stretched my eyebrows upwards to give me a look of permanent
surprise. I informed them that their mothers did not know who
their fathers were and that they were born out of wedlock.

Another story involved another Indian restaurant on the outskirts
of Oldham. The tables were set out in rows and were a little too
close together in truth. Back to back with our table were a couple
obviously very much in love. They were holding hands across the
table. The next thing we heard was him saying to her, 'Will you
marry me?' - she gave a little squeal of delight and said 'Yes,
yes I will'. The surrounding tables all broke into applause. I
slid back my chair to turn around and congratulate the couple when
my chair hit a sort of rustic standard lamp that was held together
with pegs. It disintegrated, and the pieces all fell their way.
The lampshade came off and landed right in the middle of his
curry, sending a shower of Madras all over his clean, white shirt.
I went to apologize, but he was shaking with rage. 'Just f**ing go
away' he growled under his breath. I didn't pursue the matter
further.

Perhaps one of the funniest for me, as it didn't involve my
stupidity, was a conversation I overheard between three young men
in an Indian restaurant in Wigan. One of the three informed the
other two that he was sick to death of living in Wigan (on
reflection, a very fair point) and that he was going to move to
Mexico. 'Mexico??' his other two friends replied in unison. He
said that they had indeed heard him correctly. 'Can tha speak
Mexican then?' One of them asked him. He said 'Aye, a bit'. 'Go on
then' his other friend entreated. 'Erm.....Si Senor' the erstwhile

traveller replied. Then he said 'Sombrero'. 'So tha knows Si Senor, Sombrero?' his friend asked. He nodded in reply. That's it...just that?' He asked him. The traveller said 'Well, it's a start'. 'You can't wander round Tijuana saying Si Senor Sombrero. They will think you are selling hats you thick knob' his friend informed him.

By this time the entire restaurant was enjoying the floor show, me included - and I had a ringside seat. They realised that they had an audience and continued the conversation in quieter voices. His other friend spoke up in defence of him by announcing to the room 'Sorry, he comes from Bolton'. This seemed to him explanation enough.

As we have become older, and perhaps a little wiser, this little tradition has faded out. We are all eager to get home and rest our weary bones - but I do remember those times with fondness and the adventures of our youth. I also remember several morning-after visits to the bathroom. As a friend of mine once said 'You think it's only hot when you eat it'.

Bickershaw Colliery

Mining was so much a part of my area, I think if the streets had veins and arteries, they would run black and red with the coal, and the blood spilt beneath them in gaining it. You would see the old miners. Their thin and frail faces, with hands tattooed with the coal dust that had found its way into cuts and injuries. Hear them wheezing from lungs full of coal - but look into their eyes, and for a brief second you will see the magnificence of the men they were.

I am lucky. I never went down a mine. My Dad did though, and countless generations before him. He would tell me of the dust and the heat. Every family knew a relative somewhere in the past who had been injured - or worse. Still, they were proud. They were the vanguard of the working classes, until the miner's strike of 1984-85 which finally proved to be the end.

In 1989 the gates of Bickershaw Colliery finally closed. Mining is now but a memory in this area. Everything which gave my town its identity has been taken away. The cotton and the coal. Now everything is imported. Make no mistake; these were hard industries and hard times. Times always seemed to lurch from famine to feast, and then back again, but it bred its own form of dignity. That of hard work, and hard play.

It is no accident that the Northern Rugby Football Union (or Rugby League as we call it today) moved away from the amateur game, where those with money could compete without fear of injury, and their families starving as a result. There were also brass bands, and in pre-National Coal Board days, Bickershaw Colliery had one of the best, winning competition after competition.

On the 10th of October 1932, the miners entered the cage to be wound down to their place of work. It was a day like any other day. On this day the cage held 20 miners. It was a dark day that is still remembered. An overwind occurred, which meant the cage carrying the miners passed the point of embarkation and plunged into the water sump below, drowning nineteen of the 20 miners.

We build monuments to pompous generals and warmongers. We celebrate in bronze those sportsmen who have been handsomely paid for their efforts. Few monuments of such grandeur are seen for the bravery of the humble miner. My mother lost her first husband down that mine. I have seen her little box of memories and photographs she kept in her small shrine inside that toffee tin. I also saw the wistful look on her face on the anniversary of his death. Dad understood...Christ, why wouldn't he? - he was a miner after all.

A Cabin in the Woods

When I think of heaven or paradise, I never see angels or harps or
hear celestial music. My heaven is varying shades of verdant green
and autumnal russets. My heaven is the birdsong and the rustling
of the leaves in the wind. My heaven is rooted firmly here on
earth. The earth that bore forth her fruits and gave us breath. I
have never found true beauty in any city. I have discovered
grandeur and startling architecture, but never the beauty.

The purest magic happens at night-time. When the moon's light
caresses the ripples on the lake and leaves it dancing like a
disco ball. When the sky is covered in the twinkling of faraway
stars. The light has taken a million years to reach us. The night
and the majesty can make you feel so very small. When we are made
to feel so temporary and insignificant, the wonder of it all can
only then surround you.

Throw away labels. We all have them. The one to throw away first
is the one that says 'At your age'. That is the one that wants you
to feel old and useless. That is the one that points in one
direction only.

The spark and the life force inside you was made at birth. It
shone the strongest when you were around five to seven years old.
Then you truly believed in forever. You were your own small god,
and all around you was wonderment.

One to keep is the label entitled 'Responsibility'. This one is
important as it is your anchor to the familiar and to your
present-day life. Despise those buffoons who chase you and want to
tie the label to you that says 'Oh just grow up'. They are already
a little dead inside and want to take pleasure in extinguishing
your light.

If you can keep the heart of a child and learn to forget fights
and arguments. If the word grudge is a word that merely exists for
less shiny people, I believe that beauty will follow. Tie a new
label to your soul. Tie a tag marked 'Young and Optimistic'. I
have given up all my grudges. The weight upon my own soul was
tearing at its fabric. It wanted to eat me, and I will not be
consumed.

The cabin in the woods is rich in symbolism. Made from the very
wood that surrounds it, so it is at one with nature. It is
sympathetic and resonates at the same wavelength. The lake is
symbolic of birth and rebirth. Every year the forest dies and is
brought back to life by the miracle that is nature. Every now and
then we must allow our inner thoughts to die and be reborn again
too. That label entitled 'Cynicism' is caustic. It masquerades as
sophistication, but turn the label over, and on the back is
printed the word 'Hopelessness'.

There are no secrets to living apart from one. Live your life and do not damage other's lives. Be happy with who you are, but always strive to be better. Cry often but laugh far more often. Be caring but not controlling. Be a little better a person than you dared to be. After a while, it becomes second nature.

These are my goals. My aim. OK, my religion if you like! I am me, and that makes me happy. I do not strive to be artificially beautiful. I have my own beauty and those that know and love me see it. If I do not come up to your expectations, then perhaps you are comparing me to your own flawed and damaged yardstick. Maybe you are masking your own flaws and seek to stand on the pain you inflict to somehow raise yourself in your own eyes.

I have examined and re-examined my past. I have picked open the scabs to make them bleed again to try and understand it better. It became clear to me that the pain was there almost as a comfort. I was used to it. I am no different to every living person. Everyone has wounds. People handle them in different ways. If you judge me as not good enough in some way, whoopie doo, go and find someone who meets all your criteria. We are different you see. I meet people as a fresh page.

Why was Susan Boyle such an overnight sensation? Why did she have three million views on YouTube in 24 hours? Simple - we are all cynics. We take beauty as being something from the pages of a magazine. Some people found Adolf Hitler to be a handsome man and fell under his spell. I am not telling anyone what to do or how to think. I am telling everyone how I feel. I write, I play music, and I make people laugh. Is that good enough? If it isn't, you may have mistaken me for something between George Clooney, Stephen Hawking and Mother Theresa. Good luck with finding that combo!

Small and Perfect Steps

We found our way unto that wood.
Our feet remembered every step.
Each time the thrill is just the same.
No words encompass all.

Sinking into evening's arms
we bask in amber scattered skies
and watch the birds swoop down to roost
to watch the sun at rest.

We pull our coats around our frames
to guard against the thrill of night
so we may wring each precious drop
from this most blessed day.

No breath of wind across the fields.
All senses heightened to a peak.
Soon the star bespattered sky
will gladden every eye.

Each sound upon that frozen night
is magnified with clarity.
The time has come to go inside
and bask by fireside's warmth.

This place where magic does reside.
Where dreams do come to live again
and never more those tawdry thoughts
will ever spring to mind.

The years they fall away so fast
and then the healing starts again.
The painful and the troubled day
It seems so far away.

The door is always there to find.
The key inside your childlike mind.
A sacred land of Peter Pan
all adult thoughts disdained.

Where simple things they bring such joy.
There's nought so pure as children's play.
Reset your mind to days of love
when play was all there was.

I will wait for you inside.
I will be myself again.
When I bathe inside those thoughts
my Soul will be renewed.

The Shadow of the Lake

Ever since the age of seven, I have owned a fishing rod. My
friends and I would sit beside the factory lodge with our rods and
watch the little porcupine quill float slide away as yet another
hungry perch took our bait. Even now, in my sixties, it has lost
none of its thrill and excitement, although now I am more of a
fair weather fisherman.

Fishing has been a constant throughout my life. Sitting quietly
beside the water and convening with nature has a soporific effect.
Many are the problems that have been sorted and sense made out of
a nonsensical set of thoughts while watching a float bob on the
surface of a lake.

The king of fish and the quarry of most coarse fishermen who fish
the lakes is the carp. The wily old warrior. Such wisdom lies
behind those eyes. This is the story of one such trip.

It was one of those perfect summer's days. The odd wisp of a token
cloud against a sky of pure azure blue. My arrival is welcomed by
the jewelled flash of a kingfisher as it zips by me. Somewhere
behind me the meadow pipits are piping their liquid songs as they
ascend into the firmament. I know you are there. I see the reeds
and rushes move as you nose and nuzzle at them, searching for
food. I see the water rise slightly from beneath and see the swirl
your ancient and majestic body leaves on the surface of the flat-
calm lake. Oh, I see you! You are master of all you survey. You
fear nothing. Cyprinus Carpio. The Common Carp - but there is
nothing common about such a regal form as yours.

You also know I am there because your wisdom is legendary. With as
little noise as I can muster, I set down my chair and tackle up my
rod. I hear a sound like someone pulling a wellington boot out of
the sloppy mud as you suck aquatic insects from the sides of the
rushes. You are almost mocking me.

I prepare myself to meet your awe. I cast in my line alongside
where you surfaced and I waited. My heart thudding in my chest and
ticking away the seconds. The line tightens, and the rod tip pulls
around. Is this you??? Through the buckling and lunging rod tip, I
can sense it is one of your younger brethren. I draw him to his
surrender and into the waiting landing net. The hook is removed,
and this young, brave warrior is free once more. 'You fought well
young master, now bring forth your Lord' I whisper to the winds.

Once more I do battle with your foot-soldiers, and still, you mock
me by feeding right alongside my waiting hook. The evening is
drawing in, and I try every bait in my bag. You have beaten me,
your majesty. It is time to go. I throw my unused bait just
beneath my boots and a mere foot into the water. I see your dark
and ominous shape slide into view. You make an inspiring and
spine-tingling sight as you suck up all the offerings. I smile at

your audacity. An hour ago you were the wily spirit of the lake, and now you feed at my feet like a hungry Labrador dog. Yes, I am the fool and you the teacher, but at least we broke bread and shared a meal together at the end. Blessed be Sir. Live long and be fruitful.

Talking to Ghosts

I was once asked to expand upon my mother's apparent spiritual gifts. As they say on the TV programmes. These are for entertainment purposes only. I can only report what I have personally witnessed. Everyone's beliefs are their own.

Some nights, when lying in bed, I would hear mother having a conversation, but I could only hear one side of it. A bit like when you hear someone talking on the phone. In the morning she would say things to me like 'Your granddad told me that you were playing in that disused factory last night with Graham. Granddad had been dead a year. Okay, you could put this down to some kind of schizophrenic experience, but I know someone with that unfortunate malady, and I can assure you that she wasn't.

I grew up seeing this as being quite normal until other kids said things to me like 'Your mum is spooky. She said she saw me pinching apples, and she wasn't there'. I had assumed that all mothers could do these things.

I went away with the school for two weeks to a lodge in the Lancashire countryside near Preston. About three days in I came down with a stinking cold and spent a full day in bed. Two days later a letter came saying that she hoped that I was feeling better now - and I was.

I used to subscribe to a magazine called 'The Unexplained'. One week they were giving away a free set of Zener cards, which are cards with symbols on them to test ESP. There is a star, a square, a circle, a cross and a set of wavy lines. You look at a card, and they have to hold up the corresponding card. A good average would be around seven out of 20. She got 18 out of 20. When I told her this, she just said to me 'Put them away. You shouldn't meddle with these things'.

My first job was at Gardner's diesel engines in Patricroft. Two bus rides away. I had to get up at around 6am to get ready and get there on time. On my first day, I got up in the morning and was half asleep over my cornflakes when Mam said 'I didn't hear the alarm go off this morning, but your granddad woke me'. Instantly she had my attention. She went on to tell me that he said to her 'Get up Mary, you have a working man in the house now who needs his breakfast'. Not a bad trick for a dead person!

As I said previously, these are episodes that happened to me and have not been magnified or elaborated upon in any way. If you can give me a natural or scientific reason as to how she could see me misbehaving remotely, then I would be happy to hear it.

Is It a Comma or a Tadpole?

Why do I despair and become angry? It is merely a blank page! Why do I view it as an affront, and a failure? I scribble away and let my thoughts take form in letters and words, sentences and paragraphs. Ream upon ream. I have written into the small hours and agonised over each piece. I have never once asked myself why. Why do I write???.....do you know, I have no idea!

As a young man, I thought that I could help to change the world. I thought that people would read my words and be inspired. I felt myself a sort of sage. All young men know all the answers, but it is only with age you realise that in truth, you know nothing. The number of times I have started a sentence with 'All you have to do is...' I couldn't see in anything but black and white, I couldn't look at the greys. I didn't even KNOW that there were colours, and even then, a million shades of blue.

I danced cheek to cheek with naivete and didn't even see or feel it. I mistakenly thought my dance partner was called 'Genius'. I also did many a foxtrot with 'Stupidity' and 'Immaturity'. I still do, in fact! So, I didn't change the world. When I look back at it, the world stayed just the same, and I adapted to fit in better. I then did the cheapest thing of all. I wrote to impress.

When graceful stanzas and elegant chapters trip forth, they can bring with them such a buffoonery, that one slip, one incorrectly spelt word, and it can see you fall flat upon the floor in a puddle of your own pomposity. I just write through habit. I write because I just do. It gives me salvation and shame in equal measures. I write because I want to tell people who I am - and probably so they see something better than what I paint. I want people to think that I actually can change the world, but I hope to Christ they don't listen to me and try.

I blow smoke into people's minds. I am a mark on the laundered and starched soul. I am a word condom. I am who and what I am at that moment in the day. The only heroic battles I have ever fought are getting a drink at a crowded bar. I write about answers in an ideal world, but the world is far from perfect, and my answers are just childish suppositions. Maybe a blank page isn't such a bad thing after all? Perhaps I should find the very, very centre of the page, and in that centre write the very tiniest question mark. It would probably be the most genuine thing I have ever written.

I Love You

Tell me what there is out there.
Is there an everlasting life?
Will all siblings reunite?
Will the widower find his wife?
Love it is so very strong.
These earthly bonds that bind us tight.
Will enemies see eye to eye?
Will deadly foes no longer fight?
I have loved so very much
with love that's true and very deep.
Does love go on when we pass over?
For that is one thing I would keep.
All earthly things they matter not.
All triumphs pale and fall away.
When my sacred light goes out
and I say goodbye on that sad day.
Love may survive and carry on
and it may blossom and survive.
There is the chance that it may NOT
So I'll say 'I love you' whilst alive.

Now for a little bit of comedy. May I introduce some of the characters I have created...

Albert the Magnificent - A Lancastrian Tale

Albert loved his whippets (which I am sure is illegal - but we will gloss over that!). He would take them for walks every day. 'Run my beauties, run free' he would shout, as he watched their athletic frames sprint effortlessly around the food aisles inside Aldi. Even though the manager had obtained a restraining order, Albert saw it as a right. 'I fought a war so that mankind can be free' he said to the irate manager. 'You are bonkers mate' the manager said to him, before going on to say 'and put some clothes on. You are upsetting the customers - don't make me call the police again'. Albert knew that the police had long since given up on him, so he collected his customary bribe from the manager and made his way across the fields. He ended up at the wealthy part of town. He was about to enter into The Theresa May Arms - Country Pub and Bistro when he was stopped at the door by two gentlemen in black suits. 'You can't come in' one of the bouncers said to him. 'Why not, I'm not wearing trainers?' Albert replied. 'That's the problem, you aren't wearing anything!!' the bouncer replied. Had Albert been a young man, the bouncer would quite naturally have used the conventional excessive force and beat him to a pulp and claimed that he 'fell', but seeing Albert was old and wearing his medals pinned to his chest (his ACTUAL chest) the bouncers just politely refused him entry. 'Here's a tenner, now bugger off' the kindly doorman said, before cheerfully waving our Bert on his way. He made his way to his local, The Pint Pot And Giro' and was warmly greeted by the landlord. 'Been out extorting money again Bert?' he asked. Albert said that he had, and Bert then put his clothes back on. His wife Elsie was a volunteer at the Citizens Advice Bureau. Well when I say volunteer, she would voluntarily show up there and demand tea. She was good for bringing down the long queues in there, as she would sit beside someone and repeatedly say 'I'm 78 you know!' in a thunderous voice. The bosses didn't seem to mind as it made their jobs easier. Elsie and Bert always went round to the Regal every Saturday to play bingo, even though Mr Rani regularly had to remind them that it was now an Indian restaurant, and hadn't been a bingo hall since 1997. Mr Rani was always cheerful about it and didn't seem to mind their casual racism. 'We will all be old one day - but shoot me if I end up like that' he was fond of saying. He would bring out plastic containers of food for them and tell them that it was Lancashire Hotpot. Albert passed away one night in his sleep. He had died through drink. Elsie shot him with his service revolver one night while off her face on Gin. 'I thought he was a German' she told the judge. Elsie passed away shortly after that. The manager of Aldi was convinced that he could hear the scurrying feet of sprinting whippets inside his store on quiet evenings. He became a devout born-again Christian after that. A plaque was erected inside the citizen's advice bureau that had Elsie's favourite saying of 'I'm 78 you know' in remembrance. The whippets went to a middle-class couple in the better part of town. Now on dark and stormy evenings, it is said that Bert's naked ghost still walks abroad on the country lanes in and around The Theresa May Arms -

Country Pub and Bistro. His wedding tackle is reported to sound like a set of wind chimes inside a sock, as it flaps freely in the wind and slaps against his thigh.

Albert's Abduction

Albert was out with his whippets on a lonely stretch of moorland
up in the hills of Lancashire. The night was beginning to fall,
and the hills took on a remote and an eerie feel to them. Albert
pulled up the collar of his mac and headed for home. As he rounded
a bend in the cinder track across the moors beside the old black
pudding works, he saw a light in the sky. 'Well, tickle my arse
with a feather duster. I reckon that's one o' them theer UFO's'
Albert said to his whippets. The light began to get closer, and he
could see the distinct, saucer-shaped outline. Albert didn't like
the idea of alien beings wandering abroad in the Lancashire hills.
'These buggers want sorting' he mumbled through gritted teeth.
Occasionally, a beam of light would shine down onto the ground
from the UFO. The humming noise grew louder, and Albert could feel
the static electricity crackling in the air 'Switch that light off
you big, daft, flash alien bastards. You are frightening mi
whippets' Albert yelled at the spacecraft, while rapidly jerking
two fingers in the air at it. The aliens, being aliens, had very
advanced technology. The could work out the local language from
the geo-location software they had on board. This allowed them to
talk in the language of wherever they were in the galaxy. 'Eyup mi
owd fettler, we come in peace tha knows' the call came from the
spacecraft and boomed and resounded across the hills. 'Well, tha
can eff off back to where tha came from. Get thi o'er to Yorkshire
un maul about wi' them daft buggers' Albert replied. No sooner had
Albert said these words, there came a blinding flash of light.
Albert was rendered unconscious immediately. When he recovered
consciousness, Albert was naked and strapped face down to a cold,
metal table. He was surrounded by small, grey, humanoid creatures
with large, black, almond-shaped eyes. It gave Albert quite a
start. He tried to move but found that his wrists and ankles were
fastened by shiny, metal clasps. 'Bugger me, you lot are uglier
than Yorkshire folk' he said. Then the chief alien answered, using
the translator. 'Odd you should say bugger. See this probe? We are
going to stick it right up where the sun doesn't shine' he said.
Albert let out a piercing yell, and said 'It's bloody cold - and
couldn't you have greased it up first?' Albert was then
anaesthetised again. He was getting on the chief alien's nerves.
When he regained consciousness, he had the distinct feeling that
they had also been fiddling around with his wedding tackle. Albert
was quite disgusted 'The dirty little alien bastards' he mumbled
under his breath. 'We will pop out fer a minute. Tha can get
thiself dressed. Thi clothes are over theer' the chief alien said.
The doors opened with the same 'Soooweeesh' noise that the doors
on Star Trek did, and the alien molestation crew left. Albert
dressed quickly. Alarmingly, the floor then began to disintegrate
piece by piece, just leaving one hexagonal section that he was
standing on. Albert then heard a voice, saying 'Sod off yer red
rose bastard'. Then a sort of boot-shaped metallic object kicked
Albert in his already tender nether regions. He toppled the ten
feet or so from the spacecraft to the ground. He was instantly
greeted by his whippets. He heard the message from the alien

spacecraft one last time. It said 'And you reckon Yorkshire folk are all tight arses. You beat them all'. He then heard a chorus of metallic sounding voices laughing, like those little robots on the Smash advert, and the spacecraft disappeared. He checked his watch, and he had lost four hours of his life. Albert was still reeling from the effects of the anaesthetic. His clothes were covered in mud and dishevelled, and it was almost 1am as he put the key in the front door and lurched drunkenly inside. This was the exact story that he told to his Elsie for coming home in a state at such a late hour. She didn't believe him either.

Albert Earns His Wings - A Lancastrian's Last Bus Ride

'Where am I? Who are you?' Albert asked. 'My name isn't important, and where you are at the moment is nowhere' the stranger answered. 'Is this some kind of piss-take? Is this some kind of set-up by those old bastards at The Red Lion?' Albert asked. The stranger sighed, and then asked the question 'You really can't guess where you are? You really don't remember checking for that GAS LEAK in the cellar with a cigarette lighter?' It all suddenly dawned on Albert 'Oh, don't tell me I'm dead. I've just bought a new caravan' he answered. Even after death, Albert didn't like to waste money.

The stranger informed him that he was indeed dead, and was in a sort of waiting room. A holding station where he would wait until it was decided where he was going. 'Do you mean heaven or hell?' Albert asked in a worried voice. The stranger sighed again and said 'I sodding hate this job. Questions, questions, questions'. 'Ooo sorry, I'm sure. Pardon me for dying and not knowing the ropes. It's the first time I've done it, you see?' Albert replied snottily. 'It's the third time actually, and each time sillier than the next. The last time you looked down the barrel of a musket to see if it was loaded' the stranger said. Then mumbled under his breath what sounded like 'Thick twit'. At least Albert HOPED he said twit.

The two men sat in silence as Albert looked around. It seemed as if they were sitting on a kind of park bench on a lawn, but he could only see around six feet in any direction. After that was inky blackness. 'This bench is surprisingly comfortable' Albert said, by way of polite conversation. 'It will feel comfortable I suppose, seeing they haven't found your arse yet' the stranger replied, then collapsed into irreverent laughter. 'Who ARE you? I would say you are a pain in the arse, but apparently I don't sodding have one do I?' Albert said. The stranger said 'My name is Gabriel, and I am an archangel, but everyone calls me Gabe or The Gabster'. Albert burst out into peels of laughter'. 'I know, not quite biblical is it?' Gabe replied. 'No...it isn't...GABSTER' Albert said, and started laughing again. The points were now level between them.

'So, I thought you buggers had wings, and all that tackle' Albert suddenly said. 'Wings?? Do I LOOK like a bloody seagull?' Gabe replied. 'Aren't you supposed to be good in heaven, and not swear?' Albert asked. Gabe grinned widely and cocked his head to one side, and said 'But were NOT in heaven, are we? You aren't in Kansas any more, Dorothy'. Albert looked confused and said 'My name's Albert?' Gabe threw his head into his hands and said 'Give me strength...PLEASE come soon'. Gabe turned to Albert and said 'It will be here soon, then you won't be my problem any more. Try and sit quietly like a good little Lancastrian'. 'What will be here?' Albert asked. 'The bus to the rehoming centre. Now shut up'.

Albert sat in confused but companionable silence, then a question flew into his mind 'Did our Doris survive the blast?' He asked. Gabe merely said 'Nope'. 'Where is she then. Shouldn't we be together?' Albert asked. 'Yes, and no' Gabe replied, before going on to say 'She chose not to be with you'. Albert felt thoroughly hurt and a little tearful. 'Why not?' he asked. 'Perhaps it could be because you blew her and Trixie, your poodle to smithereens.....and before you ask, the dog sodding hates you now as well'. Gabe replied. Albert burst out into tears, and Gabe felt a little mean. 'You never know, she might change her mind' Gabe said, to comfort him. 'Do you think she will?' Albert asked. Gabe just shrugged and smiled, while thinking 'No chance'.

Just then, Albert saw two headlights coming through the murky darkness. Soon, a bus came into view, but then drove on past. 'That one wasn't ours. That was the London bus' Gabe said. 'Oh, I see, a SPECIAL bus for southerners....hmmph...I see' Albert said while puffing out his chest like a pigeon (what was left of it). Gabe looked at him, then said 'It's a long, long journey. Do you want to spend it with a busload of Cockneys singing Knees Up Mother Brown and eating jellied eels? I sodding wouldn't'. 'Fair comment' Albert said. Placated by this answer. Soon another bus arrived. 'Here we are, the Wigan bus. This is yours' Gabe said. Albert climbed aboard the burgundy and cream coloured bus. 'If tha wants a ciggie, it's upstairs' the bus conductor said. Gabe waved him off and took his place back on the bench.

Once aboard, Albert climbed upstairs, and the familiar smell of stale tobacco assailed his nostrils. 'Ee, that's bloody grand' Albert said. Then he heard a familiar voice, that said 'I'm o'er here, lad'. It was Doris and Trixie. Albert sat gratefully alongside his Doris. Doris said 'Don't try and stroke Trixie just yet'. Albert looked at Trixie and heard him growl,and saw his lip curl upwards, displaying a row of teeth. Small wisps of smoke were still issuing forth from his coat. 'Any idea where we are going?' Albert asked. Doris told him that they were to be 'rehomed'. 'Are they sending us to Bolton?' Albert asked. Doris told him that they were going to have their souls and their memories wiped clean, and they were to be put back into the bodies of new little babies. A tear rolled down Albert's cheek. He stumbled out the words between the tears 'I don't want that. I don't want to lose thee, love'. Doris gave his hand a squeeze. She then kissed his cheek and said 'Don't worry love. We will be holding hands as they do it'. As the bus drove off into the distance, Doris leaned against Albert. Even Trixie gave his nose a lick. The bus moved off through the murky darkness and was gone.

Just The Way You Are

The unforgiving seconds fall
and tick it follows tock.
How quickly do those hands turn
upon your body clock.
You once felt quite invincible
on junk food you would thrive.
Life was an adventure.
It was great to be alive.
But gravity it takes its course,
each eye now has a bag
and bits that were quite perky
have started now to sag.
But there are still good tunes
on this old fiddle played.
It's just the speed we start at
it might just be delayed.
But take things nice and steady
there's nothing can go wrong.
We just need some patience
as the spring is not as strong.
Spend the days in laughter.
rough and tumble in the bed.
For, when it all is said and done.
You're a bloody long time dead.

I'm Saying Nowt

A gobbin or a barm pot.
A crackpot or not right.
Not being a full shilling.
Or higher than a kite.
If you ever say these things
you're sure to start a fight.
Best to keep your mouth shut
and say nothin'.

For if you want a bust-up,
hear my words and please take note.
You can get stuck in lad
I'll stand and hold yer coat.
Don't get drawn into arguments
is my most famous quote.
Best to keep your mouth shut
and say nothin'.

When you argue with a woman
don't raise your voice or shout.
For it will be remembered,
the buggers forget nowt.
You'll be sleeping in the spare room
and you'll have to go without.
Best to keep your mouth shut
and say nothin'.

It's always please and thank you
and 'Do you mind my dear?'
It's Saturday and football.
It's time to have a beer.
Make sure you ask permission
to avoid all pain and fear.
Don't argue, keep your mouth shut
and say nothin'.

When you're at those pearly gates
and you're looking to get in.
Wait your turn, don't cause a fuss.
Try not to make a din.
God knows what you are like so well
and he tallies up each sin.
Best to keep your mouth shut
and say nothin'.

When you are in heaven
and sitting on a cloud.
Even if your neighbour
he plays his harp too loud.
Don't complain about the noise
or say 'By 'eck It's bloody cowd'.
Best to keep your mouth shut
and say nothin'.

The Conscientious Fly

I met a conscientious fly.
He buzzed around all day.
He landed on my corn flakes
I am sad to say.
Once so wild and busy
a sad demise he found.
A quarter inch of skimmed milk
in this he sadly drowned.
What is he doing in there?
Did he slip and fall?
I recognise the stroke though
I think it's called 'The Crawl'.

Gin is Brilliant

If you want to know a drink
that will keep your spirits high.
A drink that is your friend
when fickle friends they fly.
A drink that is a pick-me-up
and helps you by and by,
then try a sodding great big drop of gin.

You can have a gin and tonic
or gin that is quite pink.
It's a drink that slows you down
to ponder and to think.
When times are melancholy
and all thinks seem to stink.
Have a sodding great big drop of gin.

When smiles are rare indeed
and your face it wears a frown.
There's no need to be so sad, my dear
there's no need to feel so down.
Pour a great big G and T
and let your sorrows drown.
Get blotto with a great big drop of gin.

When I'm in my coffin
and crematorium bound.
My liver and my kidneys
will be in Gin quite drowned.
I'll go up like a petrol bomb
with a great big whooshing sound.
Inflammable with all the sodding gin.

The Pipes Are Calling

Oh god, this box feels rather light.
I really fancied wine tonight.
I'd buy some but I'm just too tight.
Time for wine-box bagpipes.

Oh, you know what the game's about,
take out the bag, blow up the spout,
but still there's sod all coming out.
You've played the wine-box bagpipes

You got hammered yesterday.
There's nothing useful I can say.
You've all run dry, It's time to pay.
You've played the wine-box bagpipes.

Down to the 'offie' you must go.
I know this is a bitter blow.
Pay up you meanie so and so.
You've played the wine-box bagpipes.

Three for ten quid, what a deal!
I look again, but yes, it's real.
Wonderful is how I feel.
So sod the wine-box bagpipes.

Becoming Immortal - A Summing-Up

As a young man, I believed myself to be immortal. My body wasn't a temple - more like a shiny new phone box that someone had urinated in the corner of. I was still immortal though. I would still live forever. That was a given.

I was also going to be discovered for some fantastic talent, and all these doubters - all those who mocked me, would fall at my feet in adoration. I would become as wealthy as Howard Hughes, but unlike Howard, I wouldn't be a recluse. I would buy Anglesey and put a gate on the Menai Bridge and have an armed guard keeping everyone away, apart from only the most beautiful girls - and the bloke from the Chinese Restaurant of course. A guy has to eat!

Strange to relate, by some cruel twist of fate, it never happened. My mortality slowly crept up on me, and the wealth untold never arrived. But was I bitter?...well yeah a bit, but life goes on.

Parts of me began to not work quite as well as they once had. Gravity took over, and bits of me started to sag. It is only when I undo my belt and my belly drops that I look younger, as it drags all the wrinkles out of my face.

After I have 'shuffled off this mortal coil' on whichever poetic line you want to use. I only want to be remembered for a while, with a handful of flowers and a ham lunch round at the pub. A few stories and ingenuous tears from relatives I haven't seen in years. Maybe a tad unfair but hilariously accurate. I don't care if it rains or it is a sunny day as they would all turn up whatever the weather.

The stone can say whatever they like to choose for me. I never did that much to warrant Keats or Shelley. I would rather it said "Please piss the other side of this headstone", then at least passers-by who didn't know me would smile - but the price of a laugh is the same as tears and just as much good in the grand scheme of this thing we call life. Hey-ho-the-merry-o, such is the way the cards fall. As the bard said 'It's all much a'do about nothing'.

My life is not in any way unique, and I hope I have held up a mirror so that you can see some of the parallels to your own life. I have enjoyed delving back into the past and unearthing some half-forgotten tales. I hope you have also enjoyed the journey. Thank you for reading this book.

Printed in Great Britain
by Amazon